RED RATTLE BOOKS

OFFENDED SHADOWS

Howard Jackson was born on Merseyside and has
spent most of his life in Liverpool. He has had eleven
other books published by Red Rattle Books.
These are *Treat Me Nice, Innocent Mosquitoes,
No Money Honey, Nightmares Ahead, Choke Bay,
Horror Pickers, Mean And Dark, Nightmares And Lying Rogues,
Light Work, No Tall Heels To Tango* and *Go Break Bad.*

red rattle
BOOKS

Offended Shadows

2020

Front and back cover Robin Castle

Cover image © istockphoto.com / JoeyCheung

Copyright © Howard Jackson and Red Rattle Books

The moral right of the author has been asserted.

A CIP catalogue record for this book
is available from the British Library

ISBN 978-1-909086-29-6

www.redrattlebooks.co.uk

Praise for *Treat Me Nice* by Howard Jackson

'An academic book that stands out from the crowd.'
Chris High, Writers News

'Immensely enjoyable and a stimulating read.'
Paul Simpson, Author, Penguin Rough Guides.

'The book deserves to be read. A formidable treatise.'
Nigel Patterson, E.I.N.

Praise for *Innocent Mosquitoes* by Howard Jackson

'Well written, evocative, atmospheric and with a very strong sense of place and Brazil, Howard Jackson can write. The reader is in safe hands.'
Clive Bradley, TV and film scriptwriter.

Praise for *No Money Honey* by Howard Jackson

'Jackson is the King of left wing Elvis fandom. He uses his status to create a satisfying demolition of the Tories.'
Tom Watson, then Shadow Culture Secretary, British Labour Party

'Jackson brings together the two sides of one fascinating coin as he explores politics through the voice of music.'
Annajoy David, Red Wedge

Praise for *Nightmares Ahead* by Howard Jackson

'A highly original set of quirky chillers. Jackson's gift is to take something as mundane as a bus ride and twist it into something very chilling while at the same time maintaining a very quirky British humour.'
Simon Ball, Daibolique

'The writing in *Nightmares Ahead* is challenging, disturbing and brilliant. The writing has plenty of style. *Nightmares Ahead* raises the bar indeed.'
Irene Folkers

Praise for *Choke Bay* by Howard Jackson

'A distinctly Northern mixture of detection, romance and supernatural chills, it also evokes Stephen King, a deserved five stars.'
Horror Hothouse

'Stunning, a marvellous mixture of supernatural horror and unrequited love.'
Crime Chronicles

Praise for *Horror Pickers* by Howard Jackson

'Marvellous and entertaining. Jackson is well read and thoughtful. He picks at films until he finds surprises that will make viewers and readers think again. His review of '*Amour*' makes it an essential read.'
Crime Chronicles

'A wondrous collection of horror film criticism, delivers exquisite insight into our favourite fright flicks.'
David Saunderson, The Spooky Isles

Praise for *Mean And Dark* by Howard Jackson

'Enjoyable, thought provoking, informative and well written.'
IK *Crime Chronicles*

'An addictive read, insightful, dark and fascinating.'
SB *Horror Hothouse*

Praise for *Light Work* by Howard Jackson

'Fascinating, easily accessible and essential reading
for any Victorian crime enthusiast.'
The Horror Hothouse

'Jackson writes well and he mixes his own common sense perspective
with a sardonic style. *Light Work* is a different kind of Ripper book.'
Folkers, Crime Chronicles

'Concise, neat and authoritative book on the
Whitechapel murders. Recommended.'
Robert Craven, author and critic.

Praise for *Go Break Bad* by Howard Jackson

'Should appeal to any cinema and TV fan.
Complex and in-depth response to *Breaking Bad*.'
Folkers, *Crime Chronicles*

'Unique book and like the show full of twists and surprises.'
Worldly Traveller

OFFENDED SHADOWS

HOWARD JACKSON

red rattle
BOOKS

'But if you really want to do something, y'all need to mix a little politics with your love of entertainment.'

Louis Jordan,
New Orleans, 1948

INTRODUCTION

Not every film noir movie was based in Los Angeles and Las Vegas but some of the best were, and there are enough in that Western locale that when aggregated they give a sense of the Western history of the United States of America.

Offended Shadows has 40 chapters, and almost all remember a key character from an individual American film noir. There are some exceptions. These are Calvera the Bandit from the Western movie The Magnificent Seven, Lucky Jackson from the Elvis Presley musical Viva Las Vegas and Holly Martins in The Third Man. All I can say in defence is that I had my reasons. It seemed to me that it would be a half decent idea to give the film noirs of the West some cowboy roots. And I have always connected in my mind the Don Siegel version of The Killers to the Elvis movie. The Third Man is set in Vienna but I have imagined what happened to Martins after he left Europe and returned to settle in Hollywood.

The main purpose behind Offended Shadows is to remember 40 movies that do not deserve to be forgotten and remember them in a different way from normal film criticism. In each chapter a minor character from a film noir describes a key character from the same movie, usually the hero or villain. Without having a standard format I have also added imaginary scenarios and histories for those characters and sometimes connected the characters across the movies and through those imaginary scenarios.

A couple of minor points that might be worth mentioning. The movies are arranged in chronological order or almost chronological. The chronology is determined by when the events occurred in the movies. The point in time that the various narrators are talking is not specified. This can be decided by the reader.

I could have included expletives but the vast majority of these films were censored and I have allowed the characters to conform to the film noir conventions that existed. For the later films or neo-noir expletives would have been justified but they would have jarred with what had gone before. I have also taken a pragmatic attitude to punctuation and the use of numbers, capitals and apostrophes. Offended Shadows is told in monologues, and too formal an approach to punctuation and the rest would undermine what are verbal accounts. Too informal and the text would have been difficult to read. As these accounts are given by American characters, I did consider using American spellings for words that differ from the English spelling. After some agony I decided to persist with the spelling with which I am familiar. It should not detract from the monologues.

40 descriptions provided by separate individuals deny the cohesive narrative of a novel but their accounts should be of interest. Most of us have experienced coming out of a cinema and wondering what happened to those characters after the film ended. Rather than tell a single tale my ambition is nothing more than to add narrative spice to memories of the movies and invite curiosity. There are also references to what is perhaps the most famous murder mystery in LA crime which is the killing of Elizabeth Short, a lady later known as the Black Dahlia. Although a suspect for the killing is identified in Offended Shadows the purpose is not to contribute to the debate that exists about the murder. It is no more than additional narrative spice. The named suspect in Offended Shadows is borrowed from Black Dahlia, Red Rose the investigative non-fiction book by English author Piu Eatwell. In the same way that books on Jack the Ripper divide opinion Black Dahlia, Red Rose has provoked argument amongst those who believe they have authoritative knowledge. I have no wish to take sides although I thought Piu Eatwell made a convincing case for her suspect. It depends I suppose on whether you are prepared to accept a conspiracy within the Los Angeles Police Department or not. Either way I would recommend the book as a fascinating account of a murder that is a compelling mystery.

INTRODUCTION

But this book is not aimed at those preoccupied with the Black Dahlia murder. The aim is to appeal to fans of film noir and provide some pleasant memories and inspire indulgent whimsy, which I hope it does.

Howard Jackson
October 2020

CALVERA THE BANDIT

THE MAGNIFICENT SEVEN
USA 1960
DIRECTOR – JOHN STURGES

Look, that field where the corn grows higher than the rest is, my friend, where we buried Calvera and his men. Next to the field, see, there is the hacienda. It is the responsibility of my family but the hacienda belongs to the village. At first that spread was nothing more than a corral. The three boys that had to watch that brave man Bernardo Oberna O'Reilly die, they helped me to erect the first fences. I hoped the work would help ease their grief. We named the hacienda Oberna after Bernardo.

Understand, farmers do not think about the spoils of battle. Chris explained what we had to do with the bodies of the dead men, their horses, weapons and clothes. Chris said we could sell the clothes and saddles but that we should keep the horses and weapons. The bandits may have been hungry when they died but they wore hats that could get a good price. It was their tradition. Calvera had a silver horn on his saddle. From what we sold at the border we had enough money to buy grain for the horses and to keep some money for bad harvests. I swapped some horses so that they could breed. The corral became a hacienda. My neighbours in the village are now not so poor. I have been given the house that is kept for the old man of the village. I am also, of course, very old. Without Petra I would be lonely and remember too much the day we fought and killed Calvera and his men.

The three boys that helped me build the corral now live in the United States of America. They found Chris and Vin in a Californian town called Bridgeport. There are eight hundred people in this town, so it must be a big place. I still see them as clear as anything, Chris and Vin riding off towards the sun and mountains. There were just the two of them but Chris and Vin took six horses, the four that belonged to their men that had died and two others. Two more horses carried Chris and Vin. On the back of the horses were what their dead riders had owned. Chris and Vin used the six horses to buy a livery stable, so I have been told.

Friend, I stayed in the village because someone had to corral the horses and to sell at the border what we had taken from the dead men. I married Petra but she was not the only reason I returned. There were the horses, and I understood my nature. I am an impulsive man, perhaps not so much now I am old. That day of the battle I saw many men less impulsive than me die.

If I could farm like my neighbours, they might call me something other than Chico. I am the old man of the village, and they say Chico this, Chico that. I do not mind. I have a high house and I can sit on my porch. I sit with Petra and look down on a not so poor village and the hacienda. I like having the mountains behind me and close.

I never did speak to Calvera or light his cigar as I said. As a young man, I was boastful. Like my impulsiveness, it was my nature. I did wander up to the bandit camp but I listened from where I could not be seen. They were hungry and short of bullets. I could not believe what I heard. Calvera, the man that had robbed banks in the United States of America and was chased down into Mexico by the great North American Army, he had no food for the winter. Lying flat on the ground and listening to Calvera shout at his men, I understood the villagers had made the right choice. We were right to fight. And since the battle the villagers have prospered. But we were lucky and some fine farmers lost their lives. What would have happened if Chris had not been able to find six good men? The old man who once lived in this house here high above the village wanted my neighbours to fight but old men are like that, they like to rub their hands and watch young men risk their lives. Would I ask the villagers to fight if bandits returned? It depends on how many bandits and what they asked. Once a week I used to lead the shooting practice for my neighbours. Then my eyesight faded. I now have new remarkable eyeglasses but the villagers do not want a half-blind old man telling them how to shoot their guns and rifles. I used to worry about Geronimo especially as we had horses but the Apaches never came to the village. Maybe they heard the tales about how we defeated Calvera. Now most of the Apaches are dead.

We have a priest who comes to the village twice a year as he always did. He knows more about Calvera than I do. Calvera came from a family that had a hacienda like the one you can see below. He was a good young man according to the priest. Calvera liked horses and he worked hard. His father, though, had a cruel tongue and said something to the son of his neighbours. The young son went away but he was angry at what had been said, so he drank much tequila. He returned to the home of Calvera. The young son of the neighbour killed the father of Calvera. When I heard the priest tell this tale my spine turned cold. I remembered the night when I had drunk whisky and challenged Chris to a gunfight. I was too drunk to kill anyone. A man not like Chris would have killed me. Calvera was not like Chris. Calvera had a temper. He avenged the murder of his father and upheld the honour of the family but he had to flee. The Federales put a price on the head of Calvera. To live, Calvera robbed banks in the cities and then fled to the mountains. Later he persecuted small towns and picked up more men. Some say Calvera once had as many as a hundred men but I do not believe it. We found four dead horses and Chris took two. I put thirty-four in the corral. Calvera had forty men.

Calvera was loyal to his men and kind to his horses but he thought farmers were not human. I heard him say so. He admired bravery but he thought that any farmer that resisted him was a fool. The priest that visited the village told terrible tales about Calvera. Often the bandit would raid towns that had small brothels but in the villages without painted ladies his men would use what women they could find. Calvera never raped or hurt a woman or so he thought. His men were different. If they saw a look of hatred on a woman, they would tie her to a tree and all of the bandits would take her. I hope Calvera never did have a hundred men. Forty would be bad enough. This was why Hilario, may he rest in peace, decided that the women in the village had to be hidden in the hills when Chris and his men arrived.

Calvera once kidnapped the wife of a Police Federale. She had to ride around with him and his bandits for two months while her husband thought about whether he should pay the ransom. When the woman was returned she said she had been treated with respect and that Calvera was a gentleman. The woman was known to be an accomplished horsewoman. That would have helped her.

In another town there was a young priest that walked up to Calvera and faced him in the street. This young priest carried a rifle. Calvera laughed in his face, took the gun away and dragged the brave priest back to the church. The poor priest was fastened to the desk where every week he wrote his sermons. Calvera put the testicles of the priest into the drawer of the desk, locked the drawer and then left a knife on top of the desk. Calvera told the priest to be a man and set himself free. As he walked away, Calvera set fire to the room. The priest cut off what was trapped inside the drawer. His manhood burned inside his church. The young priest suffered and abandoned his God. The priest who told us this tale refused to say anything more about what happened to the brave young man. Calvera hated priests. Something must have happened between Calvera and the church when his father was killed.

Chris Adams and Vin Tanner are still alive and living in Bridgeport California, so I believe. The three young boys that saw Bernardo die, they visit Bridgeport from time to time, so they said the one time they returned to the village. The livery stable Chris and Vin bought is now a garage for motor cars. I have the dream that Chris and Vin one day will arrive here in an American motor car but for that to happen the roads will have to improve, I reckon.

Friend, it is now time for my afternoon nap. Look at the church where I rang the bell the first day I arrived here with Chris. See, every year the buildings in the village have fresh whitewash and we do whatever repairs are needed. Times change, and no doubt the village will see a motor car one day but I fear it will be without Chris and Vin. They were men better than me. But look at those beautiful horses in our hacienda. I hope God thinks he did right in bringing me to this village. Friend, it is now time for my afternoon nap. Petra will already be asleep. I do not sleep as much as Petra. Without a glass of whisky I would sleep even less.

KARL 'MADMAN' MUNDT

BARTON FINK
USA 1991
DIRECTOR – JOEL COHEN

All right, Charlie shouldn't have killed those people the way he did, yet I can't say I minded the guy when I knew him. After he set fire to the Hotel Eagle and when we were all told he was a mass murderer that carried around the heads of his victims, well, then I guess everyone felt differently about him. His real name was Karl Mundt. The 'Madman' nickname came later. Can't say I ever figured big Charlie for a German. The truth is that Charlie did me a favour because, after the fire, I was given a job in the Hotel Grand. I went downtown but up in the world, I used to say. Because of what happened in the Hotel Eagle, the folks at the Hotel Grand felt sorry for me, I reckon. The first thing I said to them was that they weren't going to regret their decision. I ain't the smartest but I can recognise a lucky break. I didn't say that to them, of course. And they didn't have regrets which was one of the reasons why I picked up the motel franchise later. Apart from Pete, our elevator man, we all got jobs right away after the fire and we all moved to other hotels. Poor Pete never worked again but he shouldn't have been working anyway.

One of these days, I said to the others in the Eagle, a guest is going to press the button on the elevator and what they'll find is poor Pete lying dead there on the floor.

It didn't happen which was lucky considering how old Pete was and that we had a mass murderer roaming around the hotel, under our very noses so to speak.

But before Charlie set fire to the Eagle, most days he wasn't a problem, and remember a lot of the time he wasn't there because Charlie was a travelling man. Most of the time he'd be out somewhere in California selling insurance or so we thought. He was doing something, and don't we know it now. I'll admit Charlie could be moody. Charlie had his quiet days when he had this look in his eyes but most of the time he was friendly. That quiet look, though, was something to remember. Thinking about it now, knowing what was written about Charlie Meadows in the papers, reading about this guy they called Karl 'Madman' Mundt, remembering those looks gives me shivers, I can tell you. But if I had to pick a guy to have me buy a beer, I would pick Charlie any time over that writer guy Barton Fink that lived in the next room to Charlie. Barton Fink was in the news as much as Charlie Meadows because he wrote scripts for the people in Hollywood and because he'd learned how to talk plenty.

That Fink guy was polite enough but if ever a smile appeared on his face, I missed it. Charlie would ask you how you were doing. I didn't even get the time of day from that Barton Fink. I don't even understand what he was doing in the Hotel Eagle. A Hollywood scriptwriter, he could have had a room in the Grand. Man, he could have had a whole floor to himself. Instead he was in the Eagle giving me a dog's life about the peeling wallpaper. We had a problem with the wallpaper because of the heat melting the adhesive. I knew it, and no one liked it happening but it got to this Barton Fink guy big style, like he was frightened he'd discover something behind the wallpaper. If it had annoyed me as much as it did this Barton Fink, I would have skedaddled to the Grand like pronto.

All my life I've lived in either Los Angeles or close by. My whole life. And all my life I've been in the hotel business. There was a time I wanted to be a writer myself but my work meant I was always busy attending people. I have stories. Things happen in hotels but not many get burnt down by a mass murderer. That was a first. The block where the Eagle used to be is now a parking lot. I used to swap stories with Charlie. Of course I know now that Charlie had even more stories he could have told me and compared to those stories mine didn't amount to much because I ain't killed nobody and I wasn't walking around with someone's head in a briefcase. Nevertheless, though, Charlie always listened to the stories I told. Charlie was polite that way. He was interested in people which I suppose you have to be if you go to the trouble of killing them and carrying round their heads.

In this business you talk to people and you hear things, and that's on the good days. On the bad days you see what you don't want to remember.

As soon as I had my first motel franchise, I said to Myrtle my wife, this motel thing isn't going to be no Hotel Grand high life. Myrtle, I said, if we don't want to be running budget motels for the rest of our lives we're going to have to work hard and make sacrifices.

Chet, no budget Motel 6 franchise for us, she said.

Old Hank Hoffman, who was also on the payroll at the Eagle, was ahead of me in moving to the motel business. He insisted that the Black Dahlia dame had been bumped off in his motel and said there were cops that thought he had a point. I know Hank had to clear a hell of a lot of blood out of one of his bedrooms. He did this before calling the police which Hank took his time about, and which you wouldn't do these days. Hank first thought the couple had just been rough with each other. And maybe they had, and maybe the dame was nothing to do with the Black Dahlia because you do see some strange people in the hotel business.

These days Myrtle and me run a classy motel but it's meant hard work getting out to Palm Springs, I can tell you. And I wouldn't have done it without Myrtle. She used to do the laundry at the Eagle but I got her the job at the Grand after the big fire. I'm not sure what would have happened to me without Myrtle. I know I wouldn't have been wearing clean shirts every day.

Pete came over to see me at the Grand. The poor guy was living on a pension, so I made sure he got a slap up lunch buckshee. To be honest, Pete looked as if he needed it but then he always did, even when he was working the elevator at the Eagle which was why I always expected to find him dead on the floor. The idea for getting a motel came from Pete.

Chet, get out of the hotels and get out of LA, said Pete.

Palm Springs ain't really LA, so I like to think I did both. I asked Pete did he ever get bored working the elevator. Pete may have just had a slap up meal on the house but he wasn't cheerful.

I couldn't stand the Hotel Eagle and I hate Los Angeles, he said.

Fair enough, I thought.

Living and working in this town is purgatory, said Pete. Charlie did the right thing setting fire to the Hotel Eagle. Send the damned place to hell where it belongs.

I did remind Pete that Charlie shouldn't have gone round killing those people and collecting their heads the way he did. At least Pete and me were agreed on that.

But the man talked gloomy, even if being miserable didn't seem to bother him none. Pete had a problem with the elevator, well not what anyone else would call a problem. But I helped Pete put a few Scotches under his belt and gave him a cigar to smoke and he talked. Pete kept going on about how the Hotel Eagle was purgatory and that we had our own devil in the place and were too dumb to notice. I could have said how we were supposed to notice, especially as Charlie Meadows always talked pleasantly, but I didn't. Instead I let Pete talk and tell me how much he hated riding the elevator day after day.

Los Angeles, the Hotel Eagle, all of it, it's one big purgatory, said Pete.

I don't see it that way, I said.

And I certainly wouldn't have seen it that way after a big slap up cost nothing meal although I didn't say that. Each to his own, I suppose. I didn't have to go up and down every day in the same elevator.

It's like travelling between heaven and hell except you never get there, said Pete.

Woah, I thought.

All these faceless and damned souls, said Pete, one after another getting in the elevator and making me take them to somewhere where they'll rest and wait for another day in purgatory.

I wasn't saying much at this point. I did think, though, of something Myrtle once said.

Every morning in the motel, she said, the two of us straighten the pillows, pump them into shape and shake out what the guests' heads have left behind.

Left behind? I said.

Something of their guilty conscience, said Myrtle.

When she said it, I thought of Pete right away who by then had died and by all accounts left nothing.

If Pete wasn't a barrel of laughs, that day, I thank him for talking about hotels and Los Angeles the way he did. Without it I doubt I would have pushed for the motel franchise or worked so hard to make it out here to Palm Springs. I have seen Barton Fink once or twice. I think he was just here visiting friends from the movie business. I heard Fink had some kind of breakdown after he found out what happened to his family. We didn't speak. If Fink had smiled or shook hands, it might have been different. Myrtle and me don't have the money of the folk round here but we're comfortable in our small home at the back of the motel and we like to sit on the porch and look at the mountains. We do, though, sometimes miss the sea, you know, waves and sitting on the beach and staring out at the horizon.

JAKE GITTES

CHINATOWN
USA 1974
DIRECTOR – ROMAN POLANSKI

Jake Gittes liked to live off the fat of the land, you know. He had the fancy office, good suits and all of that. And it was okay when he was making money which to be fair to the man most of the time we did. Los Angeles worked out well for us. Two things about this town, Mister, you should know. The rich and not just the movie stars like to screw around, and the aggrieved always expect to be paid in cash for their hurt. Divorce was and still is popular in LA because it helped and helps a lot of women settle in the hills with their divorce settlements. You get my meaning? We were good at divorce work. Jake, Duffy and me gave it a professional gloss. Jake more than Duffy and me.

In the early days Jake was not that much of a drinker. Even later no one worried about Jake and his drinking. The booze hasn't done him any harm, added a few wrinkles and pounds maybe. Sure I remember. He dragged Duffy and me into his business in '32. Sophie arrived as the secretary in '35. I liked Sophie. She was a real sweet kid, for a while at least.

Jake was already working as a private eye in 1930 but before that Jake Gittes had been a good cop and heading places one time. It went all wrong. I don't know all the details. Jake hated talking about it. What I know is this, and I got most of it from Duffy. Back in 1927 this guy with more than two names was bumped off in Chinatown. I remember the moniker, Theodore David Weaver. Theo was rich and liked to play. The guy did more than play around with the ladies. He was partial to cocaine and opium. Mrs Weaver did nothing to discourage Theo from the dope which was good news for the dope dealers. One night poor Theo was found dead in his bedroom with a bullet trapped somewhere near the top of his brain. It must have been a ricochet because the other bullet went right through one ear and out the other. That kind of thing will make anyone blink.

You must remember Mrs Weaver. She was the movie star Maude Robson. Maude was not a big star but she was what the studios call box office. Theo liked Hollywood attractions. There were a few suspects but Cindy Pickens, the girl that Theo was playing around with, was the popular choice. Cindy Pickens was pretty but she'd only made a couple of pictures, no more. Maude not only approved of her husband spending cash in Chinatown on dope, she dished out some of the stuff amongst the other movie stars. Jack reckoned Theo had been killed by Maude Robson. He picked up gossip about her fights with her husband and heard Theo wanted a divorce so he could hitch up with young Cindy Pickens.

Maude was not a popular choice as the suspect. Fuji was a Chinese dope dealer well known by the guys who worked Chinatown. Fuji liked Maude being around to take his cocaine and opium back to Hollywood. The DA had a thing going with the younger sister of Maude and he himself was treading a thin line. He didn't want no trouble from Maude Robson. And because Robson was the big player and Pickens no more than a face around the studios, the movie boss Zukor reckoned it would be best for all concerned if Cindy Pickens took the fall. Jake Gittes had a yen for Cindy. She was a looker and young and, according to Jake, a little innocent. And if you can't have a yen for someone in Chinatown, where can you?

All this was back in 1927, and Jake, like the century, was going places. Jake was a good cop and rated by the LAPD. He could read people, and for Jake the written exam was a breeze. LAPD like their cops to take exams before they promote them. Me and Duffy were not so good at the exams which was one of the reasons why we joined Jake. This one night in '27, Jake got the call from Fuji the dope guy. He said he had Maude Robson in a room and the dame was ready to blabber. Fuji had pictures of Maude and the dope. Fuji also had the gun Maude had used to kill Theo Weaver. He told Jake to come over but with no cops because the LAPD wanted to set up Cindy Pickens. Fuji asked Jake to bring Cindy along because he wanted to make an apology and because he had something for Cindy that she could use to prove her innocence. Fuji said he didn't want to hand it over to another cop who might want to make a name for himself with the DA.

Right until the day he retired Jake Gittes was cocksure. That's the word I'd use. A less confident man wouldn't have taken Cindy to Chinatown but Jake did just that. Maybe it was something to do with Jake being in love or thinking he was. Jake and Cindy arrive in Chinatown but there is no Maude Robson. Before Jake sees Fuji to hear what he is going to say, someone hits Jake on the back of the head with a blackjack. When he comes to the room is full of police and, as if it weren't crowded enough, there is a dead and doped up Cindy Pickens lying on the floor. The lady has collected a bullet hole in the middle of her forehead. The bullet came from the same gun that killed Theodore Weaver. The police announced to the newspaper boys that Cindy Pickens had killed poor old Theo and that Cindy was loaded not just with cocaine and opium but also remorse. Cindy killed herself, claimed the LAPD. Jake was unlucky. Another District Attorney in another town and another time, and Jake could have gone all the way.

Ten years later the same thing happened, well almost. I've said it more than once, what the hell was Jake thinking when he took Noah Cross and Claude Mulvihull into Chinatown to meet Evelyn Mulwray and her daughter. Jake said he had no choice, that Mulvihull had a gun and the drop on him. Nobody likes to face the barrel of a gun but, Mister, even so. Jake should have thought of something on the drive into Chinatown. I wondered if after what Evelyn had told him that Jake needed to see daughter and father together. Jake didn't want to talk about that night in Chinatown, and Duffy and me soon learnt not to mention the subject. Noah Cross died a wealthy man, and Los Angeles spread out into the valley, some of which had been good farming land. Cross was a crook but if it hadn't been him someone else would have come along and built those extra suburbs.

The few occasions Jake mentioned it, I said to Jake the same thing. Forget it, Jake, it's history.

I know the dirt about Noah Cross. Nothing ever appeared in the papers because the guys at LA Times were working with him to make the big deals. What he did to his daughter and granddaughter was no secret. Everyone knew or at least all the people who knew Noah Cross. It didn't bother him none that everyone knew, and it mustn't have bothered his fancy friends, the people that ran LA, because they all went to the big parties. Cross didn't just keep it in the family. There was a guy called Mark Marinus Hansen here in LA. This Hansen guy had a mansion up on Carlos Avenue and he threw these exclusive affairs where the women were almost as expensive as the food and champagne. Hansen knew a lot of young girls, and there they were, waiting to be picked. Elizabeth Short stayed in the home of Hansen for a while, not long before she was killed and became known as the Black Dahlia. I said to Jake why don't we poke around and try and nail this twisted heap. But by then Jake had got all wrapped up in the business with Jake Berman and Earl Rawley. All that was about land as well. It always is in Los Angeles, I reckon. That piece of land had been owned by Evelyn Mulwray, the lady shot through the head in Chinatown in '37. The dispute between Berman and Rawley over the land Evelyn left was how Jake met granddaughter Kathleen Mulwray again. I asked Jake how Kathleen was doing, seeing as she'd seen her mother killed and no one would want Noah Cross as a grandfather.

Is she doing okay? I said.

Kind of, said Jake.

I was surprised Jake walked away from Kathleen Mulwray. She had money and she could have put a smile on your face, if you know what I mean. But after Cindy Pickens and Evelyn Mulwray, I suppose Jake learned his lesson. I remember him having a fling with this waitress called Mildred Pierce but Jack and Mildred happened before the dame opened a chain of restaurants and became rich and fancy. She had a daughter that killed the second husband of Mildred. I have to say, Jake knew how to pick them, even if he did live off the fat of the land.

You've had your troubles, I once said to Jake.

I have, Laurie, he said. Looking back, though, he said, it feels like fun.

Does that include Dixon Steele? I said.

Jake shivered or pretended to.

Worst job I ever had, he said. And he said no more.

So, Mister, I can't tell you nothing about screenwriter Dixon Steele. Something happened between the two men because after that Jake always handed out the Hollywood jobs to Duffy and me. I didn't mind. The dames up there didn't bother me none.

EDDIE MARS

THE BIG SLEEP
USA 1946
DIRECTOR – HOWARD HAWKS

Nobody tells the same tale twice. Think about it, smart guy Eddie Mars walks into this trap made by a two bit detective called Philip Marlowe. Every day is how often I think about what happened next. No one believes me but it was Sid that opened fire first. Me, I like to think things through. Sid was different, was never partial to thinking. Sid fires, bang, bang, bang, and my old trigger finger has to be in on the action. Eddie was a good boss. The man had manners and he had it figured, too. Women said he was handsome, even with that small scar he had under his right eye. The guy dressed well. What Eddie Mars spent on clothes I don't like to think about. Maybe if I did, it would stop me thinking about how I plugged my own boss, a guy who never said a cross word to me.

Eddie collected people, and I was one of them but I'd been around. Sid was different. Sid was a dope with a grin to match but Eddie liked Sid. Ambition is a curse in the rackets, and Sid didn't have it. Sid was loyal. After we killed Eddie, I stayed with the smart guys. Even if it was an accident, somebody had to take the fall for Eddie, and Sid was the popular choice. Me, I work and breathe but the boys made sure I don't do so well. You've noticed the missing fingers. Wait till you see me walk. The fingers I don't miss but the wounds in my leg have teeth that get sharper the older they get.

In this kind of business you meet a lot of guys that have tempers. I wouldn't say Sid had a temper but he was prickly. He liked the last word. Sid was that kind of guy. The detective Marlowe was the same. More than once I've asked myself would Sid have been as quick to pull the trigger if he hadn't wanted it so much to be Marlowe walking out the door. I mean, it was dark but if we'd just looked. If Sid had just let Eddie walk forward a couple of steps so we could see him or just hear him say something. Sid didn't wait, and he sure as hell didn't like Marlowe.

The place is still there in Las Olindas. It's still open and fancy although now they use it as a hotel for the loaded. A lot of the Las Olindas crowd moved to this casino that they had hid at the back of the Florentine Gardens, which was a big swanky restaurant owned by a big wheel called Mark Hansen. These days at the Las Olindas you don't need an ID to stay there, just a Cadillac. When Eddie ran it as a casino for the high rollers, he called it The Cypress. All sorts played the tables. We had movie stars, rich businessmen, mob guys and drop dead babes that wanted some of what the rich guys had. I'm no looker but sometimes the babes would fall off prickly trees. With nowhere to go they just wanted a guy to show them a good time in good places. That I can do.

In the back of The Cypress they had a room where some of the hot musicians from Hollywood relaxed. No gambling, just music and top dollar booze. Vivienne Rutledge liked to go there and warble the odd tune. The musicians went along with her because the fancy lady had cash and powerful friends. But she couldn't do with a tune what those Hollywood folks did. To be fair the babe had style. Eddie Mars called it class. This is where Eddie went wrong. He didn't just collect people. People you can live with. Eddie liked to collect dames, the upper berth kind, you know what I'm saying? Marlowe never had more than two bits but he also picked up fine upholstery along the way. He even latched on to Vivienne Rutledge. She dropped the name Rutledge and not long after that Vivienne dropped Marlowe. The dames didn't stick to Marlowe but for Eddie Mars they were like glue. Adhesive honey Sid called it, and Eddie Mars laughed. For Sid and Eddie, that was as good as it got.

Carmen Sternwood sure stuck to Eddie. She was sweet looking but poison. Marlowe figured that she had killed Sean Regan because Regan wasn't quite so warm to her as she was to him.

Her own father said she liked to pull the wings off flies. Carmen was the spider, and this Irish guy Regan died without any wings. After Marlowe had done all the figuring the Sternwood family used some of their ample dosh to put Carmen away somewhere fancy. Marlowe was not stupid. He had worked for the DA and Marlowe figured quick but I still don't know how he called Carmen for killing Regan. Maybe it was intuition.

I knew you'd ask me that. Because she was such a sweet looking kid, I'm not going to believe it was Carmen shot Geiger. The way she used to stand there with a tilted grin and sucking her thumb, any man would have ideas. I know, I said I'd keep this delicate. What was she doing in Geiger's house? They weren't studying no Bible, that's for sure. I heard the chauffeur, this guy called Taylor that worked for the family, was really warm to Carmen and him watching the love of his life get as high as a kite and strip for dirty photos was not to his taste. There was a big row, I heard, and Taylor and not Carmen shot Geiger. What she did or didn't do we'll never know because there is just too much money around the babe, you know what I'm saying. Bad, damaged or just plain evil, take your pick. What I know is this, if the woman had been put in a home a year sooner, three men no make that six would still be driving around LA. The six dead? Include my thumbs and I have just enough fingers to count. Okay you count then, poor Sid, Owen Taylor, Eddie Mars, Sean Regan, Joe Brodie, Harry Jones, and Geiger the book guy who had the porn racket. And I'm forgetting Lash Canino. Marlowe nailed Canino. Count again. There are four blackmail pinches in that lot. Maybe they had it coming, and maybe because Eddie was also dipping his fingers in the pot he deserved what happened. But I sure wish my trigger finger hadn't reacted that night. That particular finger was the first the guys took.

I met Marlowe last fall. By then Vivienne Rutledge was long gone. Marlowe was just the same as I'd remembered. He still had the mouth and he didn't carry a torch for no one. Marlowe had been working up in Hollywood. He should have been loaded but as always he didn't have two bits. I bought the beers. Some old bootlegger called Joe Kennedy had gone respectable and bought into this studio. What was the name? Three letters, not MGM, that's it, RKO. The way Marlowe tells it, this guy Kennedy wanted to make cheap movies but there was some psycho writer on the RKO payroll called Dixon Steele and Steele may be his name but Steele he wasn't. This Dixon Steele already had problems. He bathed in booze and liked to knock ladies around. Steele was in no mood to be polite to an ex-mobster like Kennedy. Mr Dixon Steele reckoned his typewriter deserved better than junk scripts for cheap movies. Marlowe was hired to keep Kennedy and Steele apart. Well, Marlowe didn't last long which may be why he didn't have two bits. Marlowe said this guy Kennedy was one lousy piece.

You watch, Pete, he said. One day he'll be running the country.

That was Marlowe. The rich brought out the worst in him. I bought the beers. Even after what happened there was never no bad blood between Marlowe and me. I didn't always like what came out of his mouth but I had him figured. He thought people were rotten, no exceptions including himself. Sid thought the insults with Marlowe were personal. I told Sid, get wise, Marlowe is like that with everybody. There was no room for Marlowe to carry a torch. He carried crosses.

Eddie had the charm but he was always a mob guy. Where do you think he got the cash to open The Cypress? Eddie had friends, and in the rackets that means getting favours but also taking your turn when favours need to be done, you know what I'm saying. I don't know what his game was with the Sternwood bunch. Eddie put the pinch on them twice, so he was taking advantage. But he was also doing them a favour. Only Eddie can say, and we all know what happened to him. Eddie had cash, connections, a casino which he could skim, and his own schemes. Eddie Mars was better than blackmail. But the two dames had class and style. They turned his head. He even let people think his wife had run off with this Irish guy Regan. That doesn't sound like a straight blackmail pinch to me.

EDDIE MARS

The time I bought Marlowe the booze I asked him to explain how he figured Carmen for killing Regan. He never answered me straight. Instead he goes through the whole damned business again. I listen and spend all what's in my wallet. I didn't say before. Marlowe likes an Old Forester bourbon chaser with his beers. The dish behind the bar knew Marlowe. She was once a taxi driver, and they remembered one another. Some guys are like that. They collect dames. Eddie did. Sid and me would show them a good time but we weren't collectors.

MIKE 'BLACK IRISH' O'HARA

THE LADY FROM SHANGHAI
USA 1947
DIRECTOR – ORSON WELLES

Mike O'Hara used to say that there were no happy endings but the same man went to his bed and died before he woke up. With what is happening inside my body these days I can be too easily persuaded that any unconscious death counts as a happy ending. Mike wrote two good novels. The rest were uninspired library fodder but at least they had a beginning, a middle and an end. He produced a novel a year, which meant that as his agent I was in no position to complain, even when it was obvious his heart was not in writing anymore. His best work was non-fiction, certainly in his later years, although the American market for his kind of politics was limited.

Somehow I managed a deal for a collection of the articles he produced in the late '50s for a not too popular left wing magazine. They were good articles or at least well-written. Norman Mailer was an admirer, and I am convinced Mailer copied Mike's style when he wrote for The Village Voice. Those political columns of Mike led to a few TV chat show interviews for which he was paid quite well. As his agent, I took the same percentage from him as I did everyone else but Mike was not really interested in money. He bought a small remote house on the edge of LA and close to the desert. His place was near Llano del Rio where there had been this socialist colony at the beginning of the century. For Mike the idea had appeal. Llano del Rio later became a dull suburb.

Mike, stop trying so hard to be like Jack London, I used to say.
There is no harm in that, Mike would reply.
Before Mike came to Los Angeles, and before he met me,

Mike liked to travel the world and mingle with what he thought were the oppressed. Unlike Jack London he avoided alcoholism. All Mike ever drank was beer. His big heavy frame was like a sponge. I don't think I ever saw him drunk. His father fought for the Irish and against the British which might have been one of the reasons why sixteen years old Mike O'Hara left Ireland and set off around the world. The other sailors called him Mr Poet. Mike learnt how to handle boats, and if he hadn't, he would never have become involved with Elsa Bannister.

The two good books that I admire are Kiss The Sunrise and Death Of A Spy. Kiss The Sunrise took advantage of what happened to Mike in San Francisco. I advised against the title but Mike insisted. Kiss the sunrise were not the final words Elsa uttered when she died but that was how Mike wanted everyone to remember her. What Elsa called Mike O'Hara with her dying breaths I would rather not repeat. Death Of A Spy may have been the better book but it was Kiss The Sunrise that provided for Mike and me a substantial part of our income. Hollywood purchased the rights to Kiss The Sunrise, and a whizz kid director was hired to make the movie. From what I heard the production was plagued from the beginning. Mike watched half an hour of the movie and stormed out of the cinema. He drank a lot of beer that night. I attempted to secure a screenwriting deal for Mike but, because of the Hollywood Ten and Senator McCarthy, the last thing that any movie producer wanted was another script writer with a fondness for left wing polemics.

Death Of A Spy would have made a half decent movie but the wisdom within Hollywood was that while wars were good box office the Spanish Civil War was of no interest to the average American. I still argue that Death Of A Spy was superior to For Whom The Bell Tolls. No one admires Ernest Hemingway more than me but his prose was always unsuited to novels. Papa's short stories, though, are in a class of their own. Since they were published I have re-read them every year. That would be the perfect ending for me. Reading one of the short stories of Hemingway, switching off the bedroom light, putting my head on the pillow and dying before I wake up.

Death Of A Spy, like Kiss The Sunrise, was also based on something that occurred in real life. Mike had to kill a fascist spy in the Spanish Civil War, a man he liked and thought was a friend. Mike fighting against Franco was predictable. The real surprise is that somehow he survived the bullets and the Spanish senoritas. Maybe it was because he had dark hair himself. His thick black mop and overall gloom earned him the nickname Black Irish. Of course, with a war against Franco to endure Mike would have had other things on his mind besides Spanish senoritas.

Elsa had a Spanish father but when Mike met her she was a blonde and she really did turn his head. The woman was beautiful. Mike had a collection of photographs that he took when they were on the boat and when he was taking Elsa and her husband from one picturesque port to another. I do not have to look at those photos for something to catch in my throat. All I have to do is close my eyes and remember how she looked. Imagine a memory of a photograph persisting like that. But I know Mike, and he was too complicated for simple lust.

None of us understood what Elsa ever saw in Arthur Bannister. He was rich but so are others. I did hear that Elsa had been in trouble with some pimp when Bannister found her. I hired a private detective called Marlowe to find out the name of the pimp but all he heard was that the pimp was some creepy Norwegian guy that people remembered because of his prominent Adam's Apple. When Mike and Elsa met in Central Park the beauty of Elsa obliged him to offer her his last cigarette. And if she had said no, he might have remembered for the rest of his life a beautiful woman that once smiled fleetingly but said no, no more. We all have memories and fancies. But to let a dangerous woman sink her claws into you and want nothing else but those moments with her, well, that is different.

Elsa was suffering, and that was probably the reason she was alone in a Hansom cab and riding around Central Park that first evening. The oppressed had a fatal attraction for Mike, and, no matter how much wealth her husband Arthur Bannister had, Elsa belonged to the oppressed. I remember Mike talking about Elsa. He did it more than once.

It wasn't just that she had a gorgeous figure and beautiful eyes, he would say, there was pain in those eyes. I was born to be the chump that tried to rescue her.

A critic said something similar about his novels, that they were all about chumps desperate to be knights errant.

Mike was always on his guard with women after Elsa Bannister. Of course, the beer and the food did not help how he looked. That helped him keep women at a distance but it was more than that.

We all get burned, I would say to Mike.

I wasn't burned, he would say, I was scorched.

That kind of pain doesn't heal, and I think that surprised him. Mike had seen a lot of pain on his travels. He had witnessed the slaughter of war and seen the poor scrambling to survive. His politics insisted that there was a way of reducing that suffering. A scorched heart that remains a crisp cinder until the day you die, that shocked the life out of him.

We all know what happened. Arthur Bannister had a partner called Grisby. Elsa and Grisby thought it would be a good idea to kill Arthur. Grisby wanted Bannister's money, and Elsa wanted a life without her husband but not without his money. The plan was that Grisby would kill Bannister but he needed an alibi. Grisby said nothing to Mike about the plan of Elsa and him to kill husband Arthur. What Grisby said to Mike was that he needed to escape to an island but for that to happen, and for the insurance company to pay up, the authorities needed to think Grisby was dead. For five thousand dollars Mike would sign a false confession saying he killed Grisby. There was no danger of Mike being arrested, so Grisby said, because there would be no dead body. If that sounds complicated, what actually happened was even more unbelievable. The detective employed by Bannister discovered the plan, and Grisby killed him. Elsa needed to cover her tracks, and as far as I can see, panicked. She murdered Grisby. Because of the signed confession of Mike, everyone assumed that Mike was the killer. He would have gone to the gas chamber if he had not escaped from the court where he was being tried and if Elsa and husband Arthur had not decided to shoot one another. Mike had a lucky break. He found the gun that Elsa had used to kill Grisby, and Arthur had left behind a letter explaining what really happened.

I had a phone call from gangster Mickey Cohen not long after he came out of prison. Mickey was fascinated by the story of Mike, Elsa and Arthur. The papers were full of the trial and the killings. Mickey reckoned that Mike was a guy, these are his words, who knew how to get out of a jam. Mike was the man that Mickey wanted to write his autobiography, these are his words again, tell his side of the story and how the big guys always pick on the little man. I mumbled something about existing contracts and gave him the names of a couple of agents I had never liked. I was relieved to put the phone down. Mike thought the incident hilarious when I mentioned it. I have a horrible suspicion that he might have even been tempted by the idea of working with LA's biggest crook. I know he entertained the notion of doing a book on the Black Dahlia murder. I said no to that idea as well. The Black Dahlia will be a crowded field for authors, I told him. But we talked about the idea.

Do you think the victim with blonde hair would have looked like Elsa? I asked Mike.

No one looked like Elsa, Mike said.

And he gave me a long stare that I have never forgotten, so much despair and anger in a pair of eyes. No wonder they called him Black Irish. Maybe when you're that lonely that is how you die, quietly.

DAVE 'SLOTS' ATKINS

FALLEN ANGEL
USA 1945
DIRECTOR – OTTO PREMINGER

Poor Stella. If only the sweet girl had known. The number of times Dave Atkins asked her to go off with him to Vegas and get married, and always Stella said no like she did to all the guys. Eric Stanton was another guy that thought Stella was saying yes to him. But she wasn't. I knew her better than anyone. I watched Stella every day working beside me. She kept all the guys hanging on a string. I was just the old fool that gave her a job and drooled when she poured coffee for the customers. Me, she kept dangling on a rope. Everyone called me Pops. I hated that name, especially after Stella arrived. Me, I haven't done much since Stella was murdered. There and then I sold the coffee shop to Eric Stanton.

I'd have done a lot less if Eric hadn't kept pestering me with his schemes. I sold him the coffee shop on one condition, that he kept it the way it was, just coffee, food snacks and beer. That was what the folks wanted, especially in the summer which was when we did most of our business.

June his wife put up the money for the coffee shop. I remember the first day Eric was owner. June visited for a coffee and donut, the only time, and Eric made this little speech.

I promise, sweetheart, he said. I'll never borrow another cent from you.

And Eric didn't but none of the profits from the coffee shop ever went into the Stanton household. It all had to be invested in his latest wheeze. Eric never altered the coffee shop but, I can tell you, the beach either side sure got crowded. I warned him about the fishing tackle rack.

I said, Eric, folks don't come to our beach to fish. They go to the lakes in the mountains and round places like Bridgeport up north.

June didn't mind about the schemes of Eric. She figured that was the money he earned in his business. There was more than enough Mills money for them to live on in their big house, and Eric never said anything about sister Clara sharing the home.

Dave Atkins was there that first day Eric reopened the coffee shop. He applauded the speech by Eric but he was still stiff from the beating he took from Mark Judd. That beating changed Dave Atkins. Mark Judd was a retired cop and, as we found out, retired because he liked to throw punches. Mark Judd was one of those bad apples the police talk about when someone complains about something. Mark Judd was more than a bad apple. He was the rotter that not only killed Stella but tried to set up Eric Stanton and Dave for the murder. Judd would have set me up if he could. Judd picked the wrong guy in Eric, I can tell you, because Eric had been around and, if his ideas for money making schemes were a bit wooky, he was sharp. He proved that the way he built up a crowd for the spiritualist act that came to Walton. They arrived around the same time as Eric. That was a load of hooey but it gave the folks something to talk about through that winter.

A lot happened after Eric arrived and the folks with the spooks left town. Stella was killed, and we found out that respectable Mark Judd, the mister from the city who sat at the end of the counter, was a piece of dirt. And June Mills married Eric, and none thought that would ever happen or last but it did. It's like that in small towns like Walton. Same thing for years, and then it all happens in a few days. I said this to Eric one day in the coffee shop. Even after I sold the place I liked to eat a hamburger there. Eric was good with hamburgers and hot dogs, eggs, I have to say, not so good.

I watched the customers a lot but I never figured that Eric would settle, which he did in a kind of way, that Judd was a murderer or Dave Atkins would become rich. We know he was called Slots when his nickname appeared in the papers. That was much later.

DAVE 'SLOTS' ATKINS

Eric arrived in '45. We first heard Dave was making big money with his slot machines at the end of the '50s. His name appeared in the papers, saying how he had secured a big contract to sell slot machines in Vegas. To us in Walton it didn't seem like Dave Atkins became rich overnight. It felt gradual like. He spent more and more time away from Walton, and each time he came home the cars would be bigger and he would have more money to throw around. The money, though, didn't settle him. Dave wasn't happy one little bit when Eric said no to having a slot machine in the coffee shop. By then Dave was selling the damned things by the hundreds in Vegas plus all over the country but he still got upset over this one damned slot machine. I'm not sure what made Dave so sour. He complained about the hotel owners skimming from what the machines earned but, as I told him, why worry. He only sold the damned things. Eric hated slot machines, and I wasn't so fussed about them either.

The last time I saw Dave he had a girl on his arm. And guess what? She looked just like Stella. Tall, shapely and with black hair as thick as the mane on a horse. After Dave was murdered in Vegas she was all over the papers and the TV. So I was told because I never watch the TV. I hate televisions almost as much as I hate slot machines. They had found Dave burnt to death in a car in the desert. His girl whose name I can't remember said it was murder. I was shocked. First because it was Dave, and second because we just saw him as one of the guys from our small town.

People ask me if I was jealous of the guys that Stella had in tow. Not jealous, no, because they were young and I was old Pops. I envied them, though, I'll say that. I wouldn't have begrudged Dave if he'd walked off with Stella. And now we know he was murdered I think they'd both be alive if Stella had hitched up with him. Some of the folks round here say they weren't surprised by what happened. All that money Dave had, a man without a college education, something had to happen. And Dave was different later. He didn't act like a gangster but he had this swagger.

I put it down to the extra money that he was throwing around but now I wonder.

All in all, though, I was surprised. Eric said the same thing when we were working on setting up the surfboard stall on the beach. That is the one scheme of Eric that has made money. The night before Eric bought the surfboards Dave had called in to Walton and he'd been in the coffee shop buying beers for everyone. Dave was more relaxed than I'd seen him for some time. He had this contract to sell machines to these new owners of a couple of the hotels in Vegas. They were Italians but they wanted to run their new Vegas operation as something legit.

No skimming or anything, said Dave.

He was impressed by their operation. Dave said they talked straight. I remember the name of the Italians because a couple of years later one of the family died in a fishing accident. Dave mentioned them a lot as well.

The Corleones, said Dave.

The guy who ran everything was called Michael. We heard a lot about Michael Corleone that night. Eric, of course, just wanted to talk about surfboards. Dave laughed off the surfboard stuff. He was in a good mood.

So we were all shocked a couple of years later when we read about Dave being found dead in a burnt out car in Death Valley. There was a rumour that Dave had wanted a piece of the sister of this Michael Corleone but I don't believe that because this sister looked nothing like Stella. And she wasn't even tall. And I heard that this sister dame went through men like nobody's business and nothing ever happened to any of them. So what do I think happened to Dave? I go along with what Eric thinks. Dave was spending more and more time in Vegas. Eric reckoned Dave heard or saw something he shouldn't have and with those kinds of people they like to have secrets and they will kill to keep their secrets. It could be something to do with the slot machines. I know some of the people Dave dealt with wanted the machines adjusted so they didn't pay out so much. The Corleones were different, though, according to Dave.

If you don't let the suckers win once in a while, you don't have any customers. The Corleones understood, said Dave.

Who knows what happened to Dave Atkins. I feel sorry for Dave but I can't help thinking it was the best thing that happened to Eric and June Stanton. It kept them settled. You know what I mean?

BUSGY SIEGEL AND VIRGINIA HILL

BUGSY
USA 1991
DIRECTOR – BARRY LEVINSON

I put in the years with Jack Dragna. Before Mickey Cohen muscled in, the newspaper boys said Jack was the Capone of LA. The big potatoes for Jack came from what he creamed off the bookies and what he made from his own gambling business. Jack knew the odds. Always. Jack was doing just fine when Bugsy Siegel turned up in LA. Jack Dragna always did fine. He outlived Bugsy and lasted longer than his lady Virginia Hill. We all called her Ginny. She attempted suicide seven times.

A defiant dame, said Jack.

Well, Ginny tried that trick once too often. She was forty-nine years old that seventh time, success at last, eight years older than when Bugsy took the bullets. Lansky and Luciano set up the hit. The torpedo didn't even step inside Bugsy's house. He fired through the window. The couple of bullets that hit Bugsy in the head blew out an eyeball. Don't know what happened to the eyeball. No chance of using it again, I reckon.

Sure, I know what they say. Bugsy rated Mickey Cohen over Jack Dragna. The truth is Bugsy and Meyer Lansky always wanted Mickey Cohen to run the LA action. Don't believe the hoo-hah. Jack was from Sicily but Mickey Cohen, like Bugsy and Meyer, was Jewish. Lansky wanted his own men in LA and he got them. Lansky would never have got away with it but by then Lucky Luciano was fighting a deportation rap and had his own problems.

Fine, says Jack, I'll pull the plough for Mickey.

Lansky may have been a cold fish but one thing he knew,

and Jack realised, was how to make money. The tub of ice cream got bigger, and everybody had more scoops. All Bugsy had to do was keep his nose clean. But the Bugsy nose was never out of the LA papers. Bugsy knew George Raft, and Raft knew movie stars. Bugsy liked to throw parties. George brought the movie stars along. Bugsy first met Ginny in New York, so I heard. By the time Ginny met Bugsy, the dame was making too much money working for the wise guys to be interested in movie making. Ginny found out things for mobsters and passed on stuff. She was like Mata Hari, I guess, except she swapped more than secrets. She'd go the races and sucker guys into making big bets that the bookies knew would lose. She'd also lay on bets to clean crooked money. Virginia Hill was a busy lady.

Bugsy was handsome. He looked like a bulked up version of that writer. The guy that had the Irish name. That's right, Scott Fitzgerald. After Bugsy died, there was a piece in the paper about how Bugsy was a real life version of this character that the guy with the Irish name had invented. That's right, a real life Gatsby. I wouldn't know. Books, I don't read.

Ginny was not as pretty as Bugsy. Not in my opinion and not considering what you saw every day on the sidewalks of LA. Some would say curvy but to me she was short and dumpy. Ginny looked a little like that actress that came along later, Mercedes McCambridge. Prettier than her but nobody ever thought Mercedes was a looker. Ginny, though, was smart and she had a way with her. If you didn't know she was banging mob guys five at a time, you'd think she came from a top drawer family. Ginny could put on the voice, and so at times could Bugsy although he saved that for his movie friends. Nobody talked with apples in the mouth in front of the guys. Ginny was a hooker that could handle herself around the mob, and Bugsy was a tough guy enforcer for Lansky. Bugsy was better at throwing punches than looking after business. He should have stuck to the protection racket. The guy was burning the barrows of market traders when he was thirteen years old.

But the phoney charm of Bugsy and Ginny kidded the movie stars.

Jack Dragna had it right. Bugsy and Ginny were too much of an item. They thought they could mix the business with how they had fun or something. With Joe Epstein and Rocco Fischetti it had been different for Ginny. Epstein was queer, although no one said that to his face, and Fischetti was married. Those guys only wanted Ginny to oil their rackets. Epstein and Fischetti knew how to handle her. They said who she had to screw but not who she couldn't.

Sure, Bugsy slept around but the poor sap still had to know what Ginny was doing. A private eye called Jake Gittes was hired to watch Ginny and tell Bugsy everything she did. Gittes had tried to nail the very rich Noah Cross and later was involved in something serious with wealthy oilman Earl Rawley. But Bugsy paid top dollar, and Gittes took on the work although I reckon he gave it to one of his partners. Well before Bugsy and Gittes arrived on the scene, Ginny gave Fischetti and some of his men blow jobs one after the other. Poor Mrs Fischetti had to watch. Jack told me that tale and, I admit, he thought Virginia Hill was pure poison. His point was this. How many females work with their men doing what we do? Bonnie and Clyde ended well, didn't it? There was that other couple that robbed banks. She was a markswoman working in a circus. No, I can't remember their names. Laurie and Bart maybe. Lansky, Luciano and Jack Dragna, all preached the same thing. The woman is there for the little ones. Bugsy, though, had to meet Virginia Hill.

But Jack once said something about Bugsy that surprised me. He said, sure, Ginny had the brain and talked the talk but the flaw was always in Bugsy.

He took women too seriously, said Jack. He would have always wanted one close.

I would never have figured it that way. I relied on Jack Dragna. He usually had it right. Do we have to talk about Vegas? I know what you're going to say. Was Bugsy a dreamer or did he have to build the Flamingo Hotel because Ginny was screwing around with what was inside his head. Me, I never did like Vegas.

That dry air did my throat. Meyer Lansky offered me a weekend at the Flamingo, gave me tickets for a Saturday night show that had Xavier Cugat as top of the bill. I took the tickets because that is what you did with Lansky but I stayed in LA. Xavier Cugat? I have more rhythm than that Brazilian phoney.

All right, I'll get there. First, there was no Bugsy Siegel vision of Vegas. And there was a lot more than horses and cowboys when Bugsy dropped down in Nevada. He never did pick a piece of desert and say this was going to be the site of a fabulous hotel. The Flamingo was already being built when Bugsy arrived in town. Some dude of a developer called William R Wilkerson had hit upon the idea of opening a fancy hotel. Wilkerson owned The Hollywood Reporter, so he had somewhere to advertise. Imagine it, one big real estate development being run by a guy that should have stuck to movie gossip and a gangster that thought best with his muscles. And, if that was not damned risky enough, there was a fast talking hooker poking her nose in. Wilkerson was out of his depth, and Bugsy kept demanding more building work and alterations. Some hick told me that Ginny was banging the architect and Bugsy asked for the rebuilds just to annoy the guy. Others said Ginny made Bugsy feel such a poor sap he needed a monument.

Jack Dragna never bought any of it. What started as a million dollar project cost, can you believe this, six million smackeroos. Neither could Meyer Lansky. Luciano was really peeved. For a while Whit Sterling was the accountant on the project. Whit was a good looking guy and smart too with a fine place up in Lake Tahoe. But Whit had this yen for some dame that headed for Mexico and who had taken forty thousand dollars of his not so hard earned cash. If Whit Sterling had stayed around to watch the accounts, it might have been different for Bugsy but Whit went and quit. I heard that Whit Sterling took back this dame. She said sorry and shucks and, guess what, the dame later plugs Whit. If Whit had stayed out of Mexico, he could have prevented two of the six million finding its way into a Swiss bank.

There are three theories but I like Jack's the best. Theory one is that Ginny siphoned off the two million herself. Number two is that it was just Bugsy. And three is that the pair of them did it together. Jack voted for number three and added his own twist. Bugsy interfered in the building work and was always asking for more and more because you can't skim two million off one million but if you can drive up the costs to four million then you have potential. You get what I'm saying? Jack and no one I know has ever worked out how Lansky and his boys found out about the Swiss account but they did. Take my word, ignore what the others say, it was all about the two million. The opening of the Flamingo Hotel had been a disaster because the rain poured down. In Nevada, I ask you. But the Flamingo reopened and was making money for Bugsy and the boys, not six million, but a profit. The cost of building the hotel could have been regarded as bygones but there was always that two million. Lansky and Bugsy went way back but two million is a lot of ice to cut. Ginny was hiding in Paris when Bugsy was shot. She paid the money back to the mob two weeks later. Jack Dragna had it all figured. No, I don't want to see pictures of how the Flamingo looks these days.

SERGEANT JOE TEAGUE

MOB CITY
USA 2013
DIRECTORS – FRANK DARABONT, GUY FERLAND

I didn't always look like a lawyer. Back in the '40s I had a lot more hair and either the suits were more expensive or they hung better in those days. Of course I remember Joe Teague. And I heard about his death the day after it happened. Joe died in his bed. I am pleased for him and I like to think that I played my part in his gentle ending. Jasmine phoned me with the news. She said they had settled down in this small town north of LA, a place called Bridgeport. Joe bought this garage off some deaf and dumb guy who used the money to come to LA. The previous owner of the garage was this private eye who had been killed in a police roadblock. Listening to Jasmine, I had this fear that Joe had walked into trouble yet again. But, according to Jasmine, life was quiet in Bridgeport. The two of them settled and had a couple of kids. Joe would take the kids up to the lakes and the mountains. After that, Jasmine and Joe would guide tourists out on the hiking trails around there. I had to ask about how they managed for money. It is how I am. They were comfortable, said Jasmine.

There was a time when Joe and myself were like brothers. Detective Joe Teague not only stopped more than one interested Japanese soldier from sharing my last breath, Joe changed the way I thought about animals. This might not make sense. Joe returned home from the war a wild creature, a two fisted gun slinging brute. We all changed out there. Joe Teague was the kind of man that had to look out for people. Without him I would be dead and so would the rest of our troop. War and that kind of responsibility will do something to a man and especially one who was good with his fists. And those memories are now why I have a soft spot for animals. Even the savage creatures have a soul. Sensitivity is not the exclusive property of the gentle. When Joe hit people they stayed on the floor for some time afterwards. But he had a heart, and it responded to other people. At some point when he was fighting for the flag and country that heart began to bleed. It bled inside him for the rest of his life. Bleeding or not he lived a lot longer than I thought he might.

My old boss Mickey Cohen had something in common with Joe Teague which is odd considering Mickey was in the Mob and Joe worked for LAPD. Mickey was also hot tempered but he had a heart. He liked people and wanted to be liked but enemies for Mickey were not people. And what Mickey did to his enemies I do not like to remember. Joe may have been good with his fists but all he was interested in was Jasmine and being left alone. Mickey wanted money and celebrity. Mix brutality and excess ambition and the bubbling coloured froth that comes out of the top of the chemical jar is pure distilled sadism. Hearts are not everything, I'm afraid. Joe was a different kind of man to Mickey.

Jasmine Fontaine was a handsome woman. Fontaine was the name she used when I knew her. She reminded me of a movie star, as pretty as any of them. The war finished, and Joe was a troubled man. I do not sleep that well myself but Joe had serious nightmares. He would wake up and think a Japanese had jumped in his foxhole. That started in the war. What Jasmine intended as an affectionate snuggle in the middle of the night Joe mistook for murderous intent. Joe was always quick to react. Jasmine was hurt a couple of times and even on the good nights she was missing sleep. Joe and Jasmine split and lived separate lives the rest of the time they were in LA. This was bad news for both Joe and Jasmine. Joe became a bear with a sore head, and Jasmine went out to earn a living taking photographs. She hooked up with low life Heckey Nash. The low life was working as a comic in some strip joint and on the lookout for extra cash. Everyone now knows that Bugsy Seigel killed Abe Greenberg. Jasmine, though, had photographs of what happened. Don't ask me how Jasmine and Heckey were at the scene but they were. Heckey Nash decides to ask Siegel for fifty thousand dollars in exchange for the pictures. The cash we arrange to hand over to Nash but the arrangements are complicated. Bugsy wants to be sure the pictures are authentic, and Nash wants to stay alive. Nash asks Joe Teague to attend as protection. The money is paid to Nash but Joe decides it would be best for all if he shoots Nash. This he does, and to the surprise of Ned Hoffman, who was there on behalf of Bugsy, Joe returns the money. I know all this because afterwards it was my job to speak to Joe and offer him work with my employers. Joe said no. This baffled Bugsy and Cohen. I was surprised myself. The war left me what some people call philosophical. Those people paid top dollar, and I thought what the hell. Not everything that is illegal is criminal, I told myself. The problem is competition in illegal activities leads to criminal behaviour. You know the kind of thing, murder and torture. One of the advantages of being a lawyer is that you can be ambitious without being competitive.

I understood right away why Joe had killed Hector Nash. This particular puzzle had a two word answer, Jasmine Fontaine. Joe Teague was not the man to beat you to the end of a crossword but he had an instinct for survival. Joe reckoned that Bugsy would not only be sore about losing fifty thousand dollars but Bugsy would have his revenge by killing Nash and Jasmine. Emotionally for him it would have been complicated, killing a man, but that would have been the reasoning of Sergeant Joe Teague.

I have a theory about Joe Teague, Jasmine and Bugsy Seigel. While Joe Teague was alive I would not have shared this with anyone. But now Bugsy, Ginny, Mickey and Joe are all dead. And Jasmine has outlived them all which for a while back in LA in 1947 was far from likely. I put my theory to Joe Teague, and he did not tell me I was mistaken. What he said was nothing but I knew.

Hector Nash was a nobody but his gross estimation of his ability led to the death of Bugsy Siegel. Nash had a partner in his deal to blackmail Bugsy. Iddo Goldberg was low-life like Nash. Thanks to Joe the fifty thousand dollars which Nash and Goldberg had assumed would at least let them live rent free for a few years was now heading towards Vegas and The Flamingo investment fund. Hector was dead but rather than be relieved at being alive Iddo was disgruntled. Iddo felt that he was owed the money by Jasmine and he threatened to kill her unless she found fifty thousand dollars. Her only option was to go to Mickey Cohen and tell him about the extra set of prints she had and ask for fifty thousand dollars for the prints, the market value of which had already been established with Hector. Another swap was arranged, this time in Union, our train station here in LA. Jasmine headed to the locker where she had stored the extra prints. But Joe had heard about the swap. He was waiting. He had the prints and had also brought along a few policemen for support. Joe handed over the prints and let Bugsy's men take the fifty thousand dollars. The police presence prevented a shooting. Joe put Jasmine on a train and told her to travel a long way from LA.

It should have ended there but Bugsy, who was under pressure himself at the time because of what was happening in Vegas, wanted vengeance. Bugsy and friends found Joe and gave him a beating and made it clear that Jasmine was now a target. Jasmine may have been out of LA but Joe decided that there was only one way she would be safe. The night of his beating Joe took a shotgun, went to where Bugsy lived, stood outside the window and put nine bullets inside Bugsy. I think a couple missed. I arrived at the crime scene not long after the cops. I said nothing but I knew as soon as Joe walked into the room. Bugsy lay dead on the sofa, and one of his eyes was stuck to the carpet. Joe was like a brother to me. If anyone should know when he is pretending to be shocked, it is me. The police, the press, the public, Jack Dragna, everyone except me, assumed that Siegel had been killed on the orders of the Syndicate. No doubt they were thinking about it because Bugsy had put six million of Syndicate money into the hotel. But Joe was one step ahead of them. And there he is, lying in his grave and wondering just how did he manage to die in his bed. And if he is not wondering, well he should be. I said nothing to Jasmine as she told me the news. I just listened. She said she loved Joe, and I said the same thing which was true. But I could have said that they owed their lives to me and perhaps I was owed. Such thoughts pass through my head. I remember debts. It is how I am. But there was no way Sergeant Joe Teague owed me anything. We were like brothers, and he did save my life. Bill Parker is rumoured to be going to the funeral. Imagine the once head of LAPD mourning the guy that killed Bugsy Siegel. But then Parker never did find the Black Dahlia killer and that did him no harm either.

HOLLY MARTINS

THE THIRD MAN
UK 1949
DIRECTOR – CAROL REED

Rest assured, my friends in Hollywood know how to do funerals. Holly Martins was a popular guy, and there were plenty there to say goodbye. Holly liked a smoke and a drink. The cigarettes killed him, lung cancer at sixty-six years of age. In company Holly was always the first to offer a cigarette. I suspect he picked up the habit in Europe. Maybe it was something he learned from his friend Harry Lime. You know, Holly Martins could keep a conversation going all night yet always inside Holly somewhere there was a lonely spirit that threatened to leak out of his eyes. In Hollywood the girls with pity are thin on the ground although the way they are treated we should feel sorry for them, I suppose. Holly was fortunate. He settled down with a woman who wanted to care for him. I doubt if either of them was happy in the way we are supposed to imagine happiness but they shared a pleasure in taking life day by day. Patricia was so proud of Holly when her husband refused to testify and took the fifth. I know, those characters on the House UnAmerican Activities Committee had lousy politics and awful grammar. What was odd was that Holly Martins did not have a political bone in his body. After what he saw in Europe, the black market and everything, Holly lost his faith in human nature. But he was determined not to betray friends and colleagues.

I had to let down a good friend once and never again, he told me.

Holly kept working despite taking the fifth. He was luckier than most. It helped him that his writing ability was no more than modest. Before he came to Hollywood he wrote some

Western novels. In those days the American public wanted thin paperbacks. Forty thousand words, a few gun fights and a hero that could find himself a girl without saying much more than howdy, and you had your name on a book. Out here, Holly never did get a screen credit, so having his name on anything was not important to him. Later he went from the movies to TV. He worked on a TV show, some awful cop drama. Holly liked talking to the police detective that they had as a consultant. They could have talked to all of LAPD, and it wouldn't have helped. Badge Of Honor was the name of the show, and it stank. The real detective sergeant that was supposed to help was called Jack Vincennes. I remember the name because he was murdered, shot in his own kitchen would you believe. They never did name the killer although Holly had his theories. LAPD was crooked from top to bottom.

Holly dragged me to the funeral of the detective. That was also a big turnout. I remember this line of big policemen with wide jaws and stern faces. Holly mentioned Harry Lime that day. All funerals reminded Holly of Harry Lime. A lot of it is in the book that Holly wrote, of course. How much of what happened is there, and whether what he wrote was true only Holly will know. The Cuckoo Clock was the only decent book that Holly ever produced. It paid for his house and wedding and helped him find work in Hollywood. If that had happened to me and if Holly really did kill Harry Lime in a Viennese sewer like Martin Tree does at the end of The Cuckoo Clock then I would feel guilty as well. I asked Holly about the ending of the book. I remember the moment, Patricia sitting at his side and with this look on her face that made me realise no one messed with her. No casting couch for that girl. Holly talked a lot about Harry Lime, less when Patricia was there, but I was never given a straight answer to just who it was that killed Lime. Sometimes I tell myself that it was one of the soldiers that chased Harry Lime down into the sewer. There were plenty around Vienna back in 1946.

Harry Lime was not a big time crook. He wouldn't have lasted five minutes with the trash we have out here. I was not one of those people who found the rough charm of Bugsy Siegel appealing. If I saw Bugsy, I would walk out and tell the host what I thought of parties that added gangsters as dressing. Errol Flynn falling for that nonsense I could understand but what Cary Grant and Gary Cooper saw in these thugs was beyond me. I do not even want to think about Bugsy Siegel, Mickey Cohen and the rest.

All you have to do is read The Cuckoo Clock and remember that those are not the real names. Holly mentions four but no doubt there would have been more involved, folk intent on bringing home more than their post-war rations. Two of the four supplied the penicillin that was sold on the black market. These were a doctor and some chap that worked in a hospital. I presume the doctor helped water down the penicillin. The nightclub owner and this Baron somebody were two men who were somewhat aggrieved about having income that gave them something in common with ordinary people. The Baron had status and could be relied on to sell the stuff. The nightclub owner helped Harry Lime keep competitors at bay and shove away complaints from those who wondered why their penicillin only made them more ill.

The Cuckoo Clock makes a lot of the love Martin Tree had for the girl that knew Lime but whatever Holly felt for the Czechoslovakian girl he left it behind in Europe. Maybe she did leave Holly with wounds. Patricia could have handled that. She had a knack for treating the injured.

I have wondered often why Holly felt so loyal to this small time racketeer but then I could never figure out Cary Grant and Coop indulging Bugsy Siegel. Men like Harry Lime and Bugsy Siegel make people rich and know how to fix favours. That helps but there is more. These gangsters enjoy life and do not give a damn about anything. For the onlookers that provides relief. Throughout my life I've tried to avoid criminals but in Hollywood it was difficult. Listen to gangsters and you are hearing men making promises that people find impossible to resist. I am not talking about money.

These guys insist life can be nothing but ease and pleasure. For a while Holly must have believed those promises. Something led him to make the trip to Vienna when Harry offered Holly a job writing for a medical charity or scam that Lime was supposed to set up. The Czechoslovakian lady wanted what Harry Lime promised, which is why she fell for the rogue. And Holly liked to be around someone cheerful. Holly, though, didn't belong with such people. He was a writer, dime novels of forty thousand words perhaps but he still sat down and wrote words. Holly Martins had a conscience.

I remember the name of the girl. Holly mentioned her often enough which is the reason why the name Anna remains in my brain. If she was a looker when Holly met her, the woman did not age well. The girl was an actress in the theatre in Vienna but after Lime was killed she managed to reach Italy. For a while the Russians wanted to drag her back to Czechoslovakia but Holly had negotiated her staying in Austria. The deal was that Holly would set up Lime in a phoney meeting. It worked fine but the girl, who wanted nothing to do with what Holly and the British military were doing, never forgave Holly. I saw Anna in a couple of cheap Italian horror movies that came out a few years ago. She looked seedy and anything but beautiful. Maybe that seediness was always there and that was why she loved Harry Lime, a man whose watered down penicillin caused kids to die in overcrowded hospital wards.

Lime may have been a small time operator that Cohen and Siegel would have swallowed in one gulp but he was more than a cynical businessman involved in a crooked racket. Lime carried a gun and he would have used it on Holly if that British sergeant had not walked into the cafe where Holly and Lime were supposed to meet. The same sergeant probably saved the life of Holly Martins a second time. That happened down in the sewer below Vienna. Holly went forward to plead with Lime. The sergeant stepped forward to stop Holly, and Lime shot the sergeant. Holly felt really bad about the death of the sergeant. The shame of what happened that night stayed with Holly until the day he died. Maybe that was why

Holly was able to point the gun at the head of Harry Lime and fire the fatal bullet or at least write the final scene where Martin Tree finished the villain Lenny Carter. I did like the scene, though, that happens after the funeral of Carter. You should read The Cuckoo Clock. Tree is standing by a cart and waiting for Carter's girlfriend to walk away from the graveside. She just walks straight past Tree and does not say a word or even give Tree a glance. That was the best scene Holly ever wrote. I wonder what his wife thought when she read those pages. I imagine Patricia feeling a little hurt but also proud of the man she married. Ah, well, rest in peace Holly Martins.

DWIGHT 'BUCKY' BLEICHERT

THE BLACK DAHLIA
USA 2006
DIRECTOR – BRIAN DE PALMA

The truth is that I rarely socialised with the detectives in LAPD. I appreciated the money the Department paid me, and as far as I know people rated my work as a pathologist. Back then just before the '50s arrived there were a lot of corpses. Not just Mickey Cohen and Bugsy Siegel were inclined to resolve their disputes with killings. The LAPD contributed its own share of assassinations. Apart from one occasion all the other times I met Bucky we were looking down at a corpse in the mortuary. Dwight 'Bucky' Bleichert was not the brightest but he was a man of few words and handsome. Women assumed that Bucky possessed a sensitive soul. I only really sat down and talked at length with Bucky at a shindig thrown by Commissioner Bill Parker. This was years after Lee Blanchard was murdered. Lee was a partner of Bucky. The two men were supposed to be close.

Commissioner Parker had been paid cash by ABC television because on one of their shows, The Mike Wallace Interview, I think, Mickey Cohen had said Parker was an alcoholic degenerate. Parker had threatened to sue ABC. Not wanting unwelcome publicity ABC settled out of court. Commissioner Parker used some of the ABC cash to pay for the shindig. Everyone connected to the LAPD had to attend. I knew no one would want to talk to me and I had no desire to waste a warm afternoon listening to a load of bigots but I had no choice. My politics are not the same as the average LA cop. My politics are not what you would call mainstream American. The joke amongst the detectives was that I should have lived in Europe with all the commies.

Working alongside the LAPD was not easy for me, especially as Commissioner Parker claimed his boys were not just battling against criminals but fighting the spread of communism. Parker and his men used to claim that anyone who criticised the LA police force was a communist. I was often tempted to quit but I stayed and kept this comfortable home. The cash secured my future, and that was an important reason for both my wife and myself. But I also believed I was doing something worthwhile. If I could not stop the LAPD peddling nonsense and jumping to bigoted conclusions, I could at least put them right about the cause of death. And the work was interesting.

Everyone wants to talk about Elizabeth Short and the Black Dahlia murder because the murder was so gruesome but examining the corpse of Bugsy Siegel meant more to me. Seeing Bugsy on what the LA cops would call the slab was the highlight of my career. Most murder victims are a mess. Extreme wounding is neither here nor there. The line between damage and mutilation is thin. All the bodies are wrecked, and lives have long gone by the time the dead are wheeled into the mortuary. My job is to analyse waste and prepare it for disposal. The killer of Elizabeth Short sliced her in two, split her face from side to side, drained her blood and removed organs. To outsiders that means horror but to a forensic pathologist it means nothing more than a killer doing half of what the pathologist has to do. Bugsy Siegel was a special case because the man had been a regular in the newspapers and there he was in front of me, dead and waiting for my fingers to pick him and his celebrity apart. His face was a mess. There was little left of the features everyone thought handsome. Below the neck, though, the body was in fine condition.

Handsome faces and athletic bodies take me back to Bucky. He was a talented boxer. The promoters called him Mr Ice. His partner Lee Blanchard was billed as Mr Fire. Lee was more volatile than Bucky but neither could be called a conversationalist.

The two of them fought in a boxing bout to raise funds for the LAPD. I had two tickets for the fight but I gave them to my barber. Mr Fire versus Mr Ice was all over the posters. The venue was packed. The only person who noticed I was missing that night was Bucky.

By the time Parker was complaining about TV interviews Bucky was either confused, inarticulate or punchy. I felt sorry for him. His girl had left him, and Bucky felt he was to blame. Bucky loved his girl, so he said. He just wanted to protect her for the rest of his life. That is what he told me. Bucky showed me a photograph. The girl was a beautiful blonde. I said something like, Bucky being protected can be a little dull and it's like stopping smoking. After a while you forget how you couldn't breathe or how awful it was being frightened. I doubt he understood a word I said. His claims about the Black Dahlia fell out of the conversation but most of the time Bucky wanted to talk about the woman that had left him.

The truth is that Bucky was wrong. Half of what he said made sense but the notion that Ramona Linscott killed Elizabeth Short is absurd. Elizabeth Short was killed by an angry and frustrated man, some chap who had experience of working in either a mortuary or an abattoir. Mrs Ramona Linscott had not sacrificed a day to honest work in all of her pampered and privileged life. Ramona was an alcoholic and a twisted snob. Bucky claimed he heard Ramona confess before she put a gun in her mouth and fired. I can confirm the suicide. I was the one who looked inside the back of her head. If the confession happened, it would have been her last demand for attention from a family that preferred she would be quiet and stay in her room. What actually happened before she blew her head off I do not know. Neither would I be rash enough to trust the memory of Dwight Bucky Bleichert. All that quiet sensitivity in a not so bright brain is ripe ground for a past that wants to be reinvented.

Ramona's husband Emmett Linscott had money through his real estate deals but he was not a power within LA. Joe Kennedy and Randolph Hearst were the people who decided what would happen next for the city. Noah Cross was somewhere above Linscott and below Kennedy and Hearst. Cross liked to think he created LA but whatever great schemes he planned they had to be approved by Joe Kennedy and Hearst. I know Noah Cross and Emmett Linscott were not averse to using prostitutes. Willing girls could be found all over LA but the rich were choosy. They found their girls at the swish parties thrown by one Mark Marinus Hansen. In my opinion as a humble observer anyone interested in the Black Dahlia killing needs to start with Mark Hansen and his girls. Some of those girls knew Elizabeth Short. I was told that Mark Marinus Hansen had connections to an illegal abortion racket. I also had the misfortune to see some of the victims.

But we are here to talk about Bucky. I admit there is something in his claims to be connected to the Black Dahlia investigation. Lee and Bucky were involved in a shootout a couple of blocks away from the roadside where they found the body of Elizabeth Short. Believe it or not but the shootout happened as the rest of the LAPD were at the roadside looking at her corpse. I do not dispute that daughter Madeleine Linscott looked like Short and two narcissistic females finished up in bed together. And it makes sense that if Lee found out he would blackmail the father Emmett. That family of snobs would have been desperate to keep a lesbian affair secret.

Bucky rambled that boozy afternoon in the warm sun. He reckoned that Georgie Hilden was the real father of daughter Madeleine. Georgie was the strongarm help that Emmett Linscott used against those who protested about his business methods. Georgie had seen Elizabeth Short in some pornographic films she had made in the rundown Hollywood film sets that belonged to the real estate of Emmett. One of the films had an end inscription that said thanks to Emmett Linscott. This is according to Bucky. I have doubts. Other people have told me that Short did sexy poses for photographs. Perhaps Bucky found a photograph of Elizabeth with the name of Emmett written on the back and the memories of befuddled Bucky imagined a movie. The truth is that I lost interest after Bucky said Ramona killed Short because she was jealous of Georgie being obsessed with the pornographic films of Short. I do not believe it. Poor Elizabeth Short was killed by a man.

I do believe that daughter Madeleine would have killed Lee Blanchard to stop him blackmailing her father about what she was doing with Elizabeth Short and that the thug Georgie helped her. The dead Madeleine arrived in the mortuary when I was at home. My colleague told me she was shot, so that ties in a little with what Bucky said. But the idea that Bucky had to choose between jumping into bed with Madeleine or pulling the trigger and killing her also made me suspicious. That scene happened at the end of the Mickey Spillane book that all the detectives read. I remember the title, I The Jury. The book ends when the temptress drops her dress and she poses the question. Reliable Mike Hammer shoots the lady in her naked stomach. When Madeleine Linscott was pulled into the morgue she was still wearing her dress, so I have been told. Something black and slinky but still on her body.

His story failed to convince me but I liked Drew Bleichert. He never let Mickey Cohen pay for one of his meals, and in LAPD that made him unusual. Ramona, though, did not kill Elizabeth Short. Those who are curious should start with Mark Hansen. After all, Elizabeth Short did live in his house shortly before she died. The news from the Gangster Squad was that Hansen wanted Short dead because she said no to his sexual advances and was always begging him for money. If Hansen did find someone to kill Elizabeth Short, he picked a man with problems. Maybe Hansen was as surprised as the rest of us when he read about the mutilated corpse in the papers. Elizabeth was not the only girl there in his mansion and she came and went but Hansen and Short are connected. Believe me.

WHIT STERLING

OUT OF THE PAST
USA 1947
DIRECTOR – JACQUES TOURNEUR

You can follow my hands and the language? That big rock is where I killed a big handsome Italian tough guy called Joe Stefanos. If I hadn't, Stefanos would have plugged Jeff and then maybe me. Stefanos had it coming. So did the rest but that was nothing to do with me. They all killed one another.

I like it here. I look at the mountains, the lake and the trees. I like to fish. No one knows what I did to Joe Stefanos. The cops thought it was an accident or they did at first. Now they think whoever killed Stefanos is one of the dead.

But it was me that used the hook and line on a fishing rod and pulled the big dope all the way down off that rock. Joe Stefanos was the biggest fish I ever landed. In town they call me the deaf and dumb kid. I let it go. Bridgeport is a small town. I know how to fish, and so did Jeff. Being deaf and dumb helps. I haven't heard a sound since I was born. I may hear nothing but I can feel the rhythms of what's around me. I said this to Jeff after I saved his life and killed Joe Stefanos. Those rhythms that I feel, they help me fish. I'll miss this place. I'm selling the garage to this family from Los Angeles which is where I'll soon be heading.

I didn't use my hands to talk but I sat and read his lips while Jeff told me everything about what had happened, where he was going and what he had to do. The next day Jeff Bailey was in the morgue. Ann asked me if Jeff had left Bridgeport to run off with Kathie Moffatt. I nodded yes but it was a lie. Jeff wanted Ann to think that so she would forget him. Ann is now married to Jim, the guy who used to clean her roller skates when they were in school.

Ann might even be happy but right now she is sitting alone in a boat in the middle of the lake, and I am sitting here looking at her and remembering.

What I think about the most is not Jeff Bailey but Whit Sterling and the Moffatt dame. Jeff said she was a beautiful iceberg but every so often she melted a little and made him feel all hot. Jeff saw Kathie kill a man. He remembered the look in her eyes as she fired bullets into his partner Jack Fisher. But he also never forgot being on a beach in Mexico and her running towards him like an innocent girl with her whole life ahead of her. This is what Jeff said. He was hooked on Kathie the moment she walked into the cantina in Acapulco. Jeff said he'd never seen anyone like her. Here in a small town like Bridgeport, I suppose I never will.

Ann is still out there in the middle of the lake. The boat hasn't moved. I can't see her face but from the way she sits I know she's brooding. Her arms are folded, her shoulders are hunched, and her head is bent forward. That means she's remembering. Least I think so. I told her that Jeff killed no one but the gossips in the town believe he killed four people, Fisher his private eye partner, Leonard Eels a crooked lawyer, Whit Sterling the big money operator and Joe Stefanos the big thug that worked for Sterling.

Ann sits in the boat and wonders if Jeff really might have been a cold blooded killer like people say. And if he was, she asks herself how could she love him. And did he love her despite what I say about him wanting to head off with Kathie Moffatt. I've read that people like mysteries. Well, I come out to this lake one day and one afternoon each week. Most times I'm here fishing I see Ann in that boat. She has a mystery and she sure don't like it.

I think about it too but the only mystery to me is Whit Sterling. Jeff Bailey I know because I worked with him in his garage six days a week. I now own the garage. Jeff was a straight up guy. Jeff is no mystery. Whit Sterling, though, I can't figure. I like to read. I've been asked what sounds do I hear for the words. None but reading is like fishing. It has a rhythm. I've just read about the British being

WHIT STERLING

bankrupt after the war. They use pounds but they call their money sterling. Even Whit's name was about money, and it makes sense because the one thing the guy knew was how to make it. Whit could even gamble on the side and make money. Nobody, though, ever explained how Whit Sterling made just so much. Sterling made deals with straight businessmen but he still had thugs like Stefanos and crooked lawyers like Leonard Eels on his payroll. Jeff said that Sterling knew the odds and could always figure out the next move. Whit Sterling understood people and within a couple of minutes he knew their weak spots or how someone could be used. So Jeff said. Sterling liked Jeff because of the way he sat and listened. That was the shame of it. Whit and Jeff should not have been enemies and they wouldn't have been if Kathie Moffatt had not decided to take forty thousand dollars to Acapulco.

Kathie Moffatt is why I think so much about Whit Sterling. How could a guy that was so smart be kidded by a dame that most of the time looked like an iceberg? The first time Kathie Moffatt left bullets in the gut of Whit Sterling she walked off with his forty thousand dollars. Two bullets under the ribs, forty thousand dollars spent somewhere over the border, and Whit Sterling takes her back. And she thanks the dope by killing him. With all his money I would've found another dame. Kathie killed Whit the night she and Jeff died.

I never forget and I always get even, Sterling used to tell Jeff.

The day Kathie Moffatt returned from wonderland and asked to be let back into his life Sterling forgot what he preached. I'm not a ladies man but Marney who owns the cafe on the other side of the road to my garage tells me I have nice eyes. She has helped me out a few times. What we get up to isn't great but I've no scars under my ribs for her to stroke which is something, I reckon. I've seen newspaper pictures of Whit Sterling. He was a good looking guy. Jeff said that he never saw Sterling when he wasn't wearing a suit or a sports jacket.

Whit never had a hair out of place, said Jeff, even when he was having breakfast. I'm wrong, Kid. That was the one time Sterling didn't wear a jacket. At breakfast he wore a silk dressing gown.

Jeff thought this funny.

I have breakfast in Marney's cafe across the road but some days I skip because I don't want to think about Marney helping me out the way she does. The woman is old enough to be my mother. She's talking about following me to LA. Jeff had a theory about Whit and Kathie, about why they stayed together.

They're not a couple, said Jeff. They're a pair of poker players sticking around just to see who will fold first.

I don't play poker, so I wouldn't know. Jeff said that Whit could be straight and even fair. But Jeff thought it would be a good idea to hide in Mexico with Kathie, and after that Whit was in no mood to make allowances.

When Sterling found Jeff that second time he had this play where Stefanos would kill this lawyer Eels and Jeff would be the fall guy. Sterling wanted from Eels these papers that proved Whit was kidding the taxman big style. Eels wanted two hundred thousand dollars for the papers. Jeff figured it all out and warned Eels but it didn't help the lawyer. Stefanos killed Eels. Jeff came along later and found the corpse. Just to confuse everyone and to let them all know he wasn't going to be a patsy, Jeff hid Eels in a cupboard in the empty apartment next door. After that there was panic. Whit and Kathie packed and got ready to disappear. But then Kathie as reliable as ever shot Whit this second time that I mentioned before. She would have done the same to Jeff except he tipped the police and the two of them drove into a roadblock. Jeff, Kathie and Whit all died that night. Back in quiet Bridgeport people talked and Ann walked into the waiting arms of the guy who used to clean her roller skates. Marney heard all about Jeff and the murders which was when she became friendly with yours truly. Marney likes to talk and gossip although she has said more than once I have nice eyes. Maybe I have.

Jeff said I had to stop a heart from breaking. He didn't mean Marney. Some job I did. Ann Miller is still out there on the lake. But at least the two of us have a fine spot for remembering and more sunny days than they have in some places. I have a roof over my head and three meals a day. Ann has clean roller skates. And right now I have something pulling on my line. This is the same rod that caught the coat of Joe Stefanos and dragged him all the way down into the river. I wonder what happened to his gun. There goes the rod again. Come on, fish. Come to the deaf and dumb kid.

WALTER NEFF

DOUBLE INDEMNITY
USA 1949
DIRECTOR – BILLY WILDER

Listen, it was not my crazy idea to go and see Walter die in the gas chamber. That was another one of those bright notions my boss Norton just had to have. He somehow wangled the invite from someone and then, when it came to the big day and seeing a man be killed, Norton got cold feet. I reckon he was worried about what Neff would have said to him before he died. Norton had nothing to worry about. All Walter was thinking about when they gassed him was the damned fool he'd made of himself. The last thing on the mind of Walter Neff was the future prospects of the Pacific All Risk Insurance Company. But when Norton had an attack of nerves who was left to pick up the pieces? That's right, me, old Barton Keyes. It wasn't by much, a couple of years, but at least I retired before that holy fool Norton. I enjoyed those two years, knowing that I was at home while boss Norton was still coming out with his stupid ideas.

Walter Neff didn't have any next of kin at the gas chamber which didn't surprise me because I never once heard him talk about his folks. My own people died not too long after we arrived in the States from Romania. Coming to this country was good for me but it proved to be one journey too much for my mother and father. My mother struggled to settle into the new ways of this country, and the more she struggled the more my father felt he was entitled to drink and carouse. Both died before their time but whatever their problems they made sure I had what my old man called a good schooling. Of course when I saw the likes of Norton lording it over the rest of us from his swanky office I realised the limits of my own education. But at least I finished up with an office of my own, and the shame is that my mother and father never got to see it. Walter told me his folks were from this place in Illinois that had a dumb name. What was it? Kankakee. An Indian thing although Walter never mentioned seeing any Indians in Kankakee. But we all know that story, name the place after the Indians and then kill them all off.

Walter and me were close but we argued about politics. Not all the time because most of the time we had work to worry about. I always felt that was the difference between us. I have no time for chisellers, rich or poor, and I think the government should do something about it, whereas Walt felt all was fair in love and making a fortune. But he was a salesman, and those guys believe in the hustle and the reward. Walter was thirty-eight years old when he met Phyllis and all he had ever done was sell something. He was selling vacuum cleaners before he joined the insurance business. Norton had his doubts about recruiting Neff but Norton was no judge of people or anything for that matter. I remember sitting in his fancy office and Norton pulling a face when I lit my cigar.

That guy Neff can sell anything, I said.

The problem for Walter was that he met a woman who not only could sell as well as him but had a product that any man would want to buy. Phyllis Dietrichson was not the most beautiful woman I ever saw. She was no Ava Gardner or Rita Hayworth but the woman looked like she could be fun, and she had an expression in her eyes that told you she'd got the idea first. You know what I mean? I bet if we'd asked Walter and Phyllis who sold to whom the idea of bumping off old man Deitrichson neither would have known. That's what salespeople are like, one step ahead of everyone including themselves.

Maybe that was why I offered Walter the claims job and the opportunity to get out of sales. I was giving the guy a chance to save himself. My God, I still have nightmares about that day in the gas chamber. I wake up seeing the face of poor Walter, nothing but confusion and disappointment in his eyes. I think he was confused about himself more than anything which I reckon must be a bad way to go. But if anyone gives a number to the people who feel like that and we tell Walter, it might put a smile on his face wherever he is, because I reckon there are a lot more than Walter that leave confused and disappointed. I know one thing. I thought a lot before offering him that job in claims. The idea kept bouncing around in my head, back and forth.

That is why I blame myself a little for what happened. Maybe if I had offered him the job sooner, and perhaps if I had leaned on Walter more, then I wouldn't have had to go through that day in the gas chamber. You see, my thinking about Walter and him working in claims wasn't simple. True, I thought he would be good at it and, listen, there wasn't much alternative potential amongst the dopes that Norton liked to recruit. And there was also his politics which I didn't think did Walter any favours. I thought if he saw the bigger picture he might stop reducing everything to this one guy against the other guy. You understand me? More than that, though, I worried about Walter. He was our best salesman. Not only did he get the customers to bite he added in extra clauses to the contracts which of course was why I knew he would be good in claims. But selling is a young man's game and Walter couldn't see beyond it. The truth is that I wanted Walter to have a future. Okay, we were different because we disagreed on what was right and wrong for the country but deep down I'm not sure Walter wanted a future like I did. I suppose I got that from my parents pushing me when I was at school. And remember, I also had to witness two decent people destroy themselves. Little did I think it would happen again on the other side of the corridor to my office. It's like Walter just didn't want to get old. And I don't think he did but that day in the gas chamber one thing was obvious to me. Walter Neff realised all too well the price of getting what he wanted.

Think about this, it's odd. Ever since that day at the gas chamber I've never once suffered with heartburn. It could be a coincidence but the pain in my chest disappeared that very day. And it's not as if I don't worry. You'd think the nightmares would have made the heartburn worse but I figure there's a difference between brooding and being anxious. I couldn't forget about what had happened to poor Walter but the heartburn went just like that. You win some and lose some is how I saw the insurance business in the end. I did my job but I no longer had the heart for it. Once I stopped being agitated about the claims I didn't enjoy the job the same. I came back from that gas chamber knowing I would have a future and not be like poor Walter. But that was nothing for me to be proud of, I thought. Whatever was going on inside my head the damned heartburn disappeared.

Every day since that trip to the gas chamber I've thought about Walter, and apart from what happened to the poor guy there are two things that haunt me. Walter had an eye for detail. He would have planned everything meticulously. So what I don't understand is what happened on the viewing platform at the back of the train. Walter had to pretend to be Dietrichson and make it look like the husband had fallen off the train. But this guy Jackson is there. And Walter persuades this guy Jackson to go back to his compartment, the one booked by Dietrichson, and to bring back the cigars which Walter said he had left there. Jackson agrees because Walter is on crutches and faking a leg injury. Makes sense, you think, except Dietrichson didn't smoke cigars. Jackson never mentioned not finding any cigars until much later and then it was to some press guy long after Walter had swallowed the gas. But what if Jackson had told me about there being no cigars? I would have known right away that the accident was a fake. That's not like Walter. He could figure the angles. Walter wouldn't have taken that risk.

And remember how I found Walter injured with a bullet wound in his shoulder. Walter knew the score. He had to get to Mexico, and that was his plan. So why waste time hanging around leaving a confession on the Dictaphone? Walter may not have wanted Phyllis' latest boyfriend to take the fall for something he didn't do but that wasn't going to happen. Not with the lawyers we have in Los Angeles. Maybe Walter wanted to set it straight with me. I like to think so because I was close to the man but I struggle with what happened that morning in the office. I'll never forget that morning, one of the darkest LA skies that I remember. Either the smog had refused to leave the night before or it had got up early. I think I have more of a conscience than Walter but I know one thing. If it had been me walking out of the Dietrichson home and carrying a bullet from Mrs Dietrichson in my chest, believe me, I wouldn't have come back to the office to waste time spilling a confession into a Dictaphone. I'd have headed to Mexico and the future and the rest of my life. But something spooked Walter enough to want to forget about his future and to gamble away the days ahead. Poor Walter Neff and poor Phyllis Dietrichson. Sometimes it's the smart guys that are the real suckers.

STEVE THOMPSON

CRISS CROSS
USA 1949
DIRECTOR – ROBERT SIODMAK

I do not believe this. Not him and me like this forever, sitting on this cursed sofa and me seeing nothing but a pair of the big lug's knees and the wall on the other side of the room. The fingers on the clock on the wall have not moved since Slim plugged Steve and me. I don't suppose the time on the clock will ever change now. My head dropped into the lap of Steve when Slim shot me in the chest. This is the first time I've been this close to Steve without hearing him breathe, Steve is or was a big man. His breaths made a noise. There were times when they were noisy indeed. I don't suppose there'll be any of that coming any time soon or ever in fact. Not that I feel in the mood for being physical. I'm not sure what I feel. I know that damned clock with the fingers that don't move is really beginning to irritate me. After Steve and Slim had robbed the armoured truck I spent two long days in this dump, wondering and waiting, although the beach outside helped a little.

I can see that the arm of Steve is draped over my hip. I can't feel his arm but I can see it. I wonder what Steve is thinking right now. Steve never did a lot of thinking. And without anything happening, which is what is going to happen, he doesn't have any choice now. Still the big lug got what he wanted, me in his arms forever, just him and me. I wonder where the bullets landed in Steve. I can see that the legs of Steve are stained with blood, and it looks as if most of it belongs to me, Anna Dundee. I used to enjoy feeling the weight of his body against mine but there is nothing to feel now. Even though I can see what is in front of me it's not the same as when I was alive. And I'm not just talking about the clock that has been telling the same time for a while now. Everything is the same but it's not somehow. There is no life in Steve and me because we're dead but there's no life in anything else either which might be a strange thing to say when no one thinks of a wall and furniture having life. But after you're dead you realise those things had more life than you thought.

I wonder if Steve gets any pleasure looking down and seeing me with my head in his lap. He must be thinking about something sitting there and looking at the top of my thick black hair. He might be thinking how the roots of my hair are the same as the rest although Steve knew that anyway on account of how we felt about each other. God, the big lug was such a dope. He was well-built and pretty, and I liked the way I could make him angry when I stepped out of line because he needed me so much. But he was a dope. Slim Dundee was no dope but unless I'm mistaken the last thing I heard before everything went white in front of my eyes was a police alarm. That means smart guy Slim has a problem, seeing as there are two dead bodies in this place and also the stash from the armoured car robbery.

I am still here and I can see our dead bodies but are our bodies still here? Have the police taken our corpses away and what I see, and presumably Steve does, is just an illusion, something to help us get our bearings, so to speak? A courtesy to all spirits from God, maybe. Who knows? I just know what I can see, and right now it's the inside of a beach house in Palos Verdes, a clock on the wall, the legs of Steve and most of me. There is also a lot of blood but no way does it add to the colour.

My mistake was marrying Slim. I didn't love the guy but it was like he was always there. I don't ask guys to cling to me like leeches but they did. Slim had money, knew the angles and had plenty of guys who did what he said. So many times I was in a room and there were other guys there. I liked that because I knew all the guys looked and wanted me. Slim kind of liked it but really he didn't. Because of the way men were with me, I had opportunities. But

I'm sitting here dead and I didn't even two-time Slim other than with this lug Steve, and that was different because before Slim came along I was married to Steve. And before that. I'm not sure I want to even think about what I was doing before I met and married Steve but, if I am going to be sitting on this damned sofa forever, I'm going to remember Liz Short, Mark Marinus Hansen, Noah Cross and the rest of them.

Back then it felt like Steve had come along just in time. There are some bad people in LA but, because they have money and friends like Slim did, you don't think they're real bad. But they are, real bad. Rich men with loud voices except they always spoke quietly when they talked to this Norwegian, some guy with a big Adam's Apple who was supposed to have once worked in a mortuary. After what happened to poor Liz, I was glad to take the first ordinary guy that came along. Anna, be honest with yourself. For a while Liz and me had good times, fun at these swell parties in this big house owned by Mark Hansen. But the men at the parties wanted more and more, and Hansen could have done something to keep his guests under control except he didn't. I like to drink and I like to dance and rhumba. It's only fun. But that Noah Cross was always creepy. Liz, why didn't you keep away from him? Listen to yourself, Anna, talking to Liz Short as if she is here. Maybe we'll meet now we are both dead. But if that's going to happen, I'll have to get off this damned sofa. Liz you were such a beautiful girl.

It's just a little film, that's all, you said. Who knows, I might get famous.

Liz Short the Black Dahlia. I suppose that counts as famous, having your body split in two and found dead next to the sidewalk. Steve and me should be in the newspapers after what Slim did. Not like Liz because they still talk about her. But a few days maybe, especially as Steve was all over the pages as the hero in the robbery. Wait till they find out he was the inside man.

If I'm going to spend forever on this sofa talking to myself like this, will there be a point when I start talking aloud and, if I do, will

I hear myself? Because right now I can't hear nothing, no waves lapping against the beach and no breaths from this big lug. Well, at least I'm on top of him.

I'm going to be blamed by Steve's family for all this because they never liked me. They thought I was wild and that their Steve was a good boy. But Steve was a big boy that knew what he was doing, well, as much as anyone. I thought Slim Dundee knew what he was doing but after hearing that police alarm I don't know what to think.

I feel as if I know what is ahead which is strange seeing as no one should know what is in the future. But sitting on this sofa and knowing what is ahead, even if it's not much, it don't seem as if any of us knew what we were doing. Steve only came up with the idea of the robbery when Slim caught Steve and me together. The big lug thought he was protecting me, and I thought Steve and two hundred thousand dollars would be real protection. If only Steve had stayed in hospital for a couple of weeks like any normal man. That would have given me time to get ready.

A light has gone on in my head. I know what I'm going to think about for the rest of my time. Who did I want to take away the money and me? I'm already beginning to think. I might have settled for Steve or maybe taken Slim instead and the two of us would have made Steve take a walk. That way Slim and me could have bossed Bunker Hill and the rest. Or maybe if Steve had stayed in hospital for the two weeks like the doctors wanted, then it would have been different again. Slim would have been arrested in a couple of days, and I could have disappeared while Steve was still in bandages. I could have headed to Cuba and showed those Havana boys how we rhumba in LA.

Oh, Steve has moved, not much, not even a couple of inches but something has made his body slip, and the view is the same but different. Maybe that's what being dead is like. The tiniest slip and you notice the difference. Maybe something will make my body slip, too. If the two of us are here long enough and everything in this stupid beach hut rots, Steve and me might slip all the way back to sea and float away to different places. Something like that might just be worth waiting for because I'm going to be here an awful long time and I have to look forward to something. Wondering what the big lug will look like when he sees me floating away from him forever, and me knowing there's nothing he can do, might even put a smile on my face, assuming I still have a face of course. I hope so. I would hate to lose that. And what about my hair? My hair is going to rot quicker than the sofa, I reckon. By then Steve might be glad to see the back of me. This being dead is grim but, all the people that have done it, someone must have worked out an angle.

FRANK
'THE KNIFE' GREEN

DEVIL IN A BLUE DRESS
USA 1995
DIRECTOR – CARL FRANKLIN

Frank Green was not a bad man, no, sir, no, I wouldn't say so. He was a thief, that's all. And, as far as I recall, no one said no thanks, Frank, to the booze he looted and sold cheap. Frank learnt robbing on the streets when he was a kid. The brother didn't know any other way to get by. And on the streets is where Frank learnt to use the knife, and, like robbing, poor Frank knew nothing else, which must be the reason he never carried no shooter. I remember big Frank was no looker, and in his business, looking the way he did, it helped him get by. No one wanted to argue with big Frank which no doubt was why Frank believed he could get by just carrying the knife. Well, he didn't. He was shot in the back in an alley over there in New Orleans. Folks say he should never have left LA and that if he'd stayed in his home in Watts then Frank 'The Knife' Green would be alive today. No way, man. A gun in a dark alley was waiting for Frank all his life. The back of Frank was broad on account of his shoulders but when you have enemies out to get you there is nothing as big and wide as a waiting back. I one time saw that movie about Jesse James. I don't normally think too much about white folks and all that stuff that is supposed to make them suffer but the way that coward Bob Ford killed Jesse James in the back didn't seem right to me, so when I heard about what happened to Frank Green I was kind of sad.

The guy who killed old Frank died not long after. Frank's killer was a white guy and he wasn't much. We expected the killing would be something to do with the way Frank made his dollars, but no, this white guy said he did it for love. Slow down, you're ahead of me. Frank wasn't that kind of man. He liked broads as much as the next guy. And he wasn't discriminating about his ladies from what I saw but when you look like Frank that is maybe the way it has to be. No, this white guy loved Frank's sister. Daphne was a looker, black eyes as big as planets. Frank and Daphne were close, so we heard after they left LA. This was bad news for this white guy who wasn't much. Frank was not just protective, he was no way partial to white guys who didn't amount to much. Just let me remember some of this stuff. Frank chased this white guy away from Daphne and, because Frank had a way with a knife, this white guy didn't look like he did before he was chased. I don't think there were many scars but no one meeting this white guy would miss them. You get the idea, I reckon.

Why wasn't Frank so partial? The white guy was a horn player on Bourbon Street, I heard, and he, well, you know how those jazz blowers like to relax. This one did, anyway, and Frank heard that this horn player liked company when he stepped outside, you know the score? Frank had seen what his booze did to people. He didn't want his sister to be a dope head. You can't blame a man for that.

Frank and his sister had a secret, a big one. We all know now but back then in LA no one had any idea unless you count Coretta who was a friend of Daphne. Coretta was a real humdinger lady. Gorgeous and friendly, and if they ain't friendly it don't matter what they look like. All the time Frank was in LA, I had no idea that Daphne was in fact a Ruby as in that was her name and not because she was no diamond. Her real name was Ruby Monet, and her and Frank came from somewhere in Louisiana. And in case you think it's slipped my mind, it ain't, this is the real big secret Frank and Ruby had. They were brother and sister, like I said, but all the time they were in LA no one knew because they kept it hid. And how were we going to go figure? A slim pretty white girl is sister to big ugly brother Frank 'The Knife' Green. Maybe Frank wasn't so ugly but he sure looked nothing like his little sister, little half-sister I should say. Frank and Daphne, I still think of her that way, they had the same Creole mother but different fathers. From what I heard about what happened between Daphne and her pa it might have been better if Daphne had been the daughter of Frank's old man. But when just born baby Daphne said well hello to Louisiana there was no black husband in that family. The Creole mama had opened another honey jar. If Frank's father had hung around then Daphne would have been black and who knows what would have happened to the lady. Daphne could have been the one taking the bullet in the back like brother Frank. Of course it could have all been different if her mother had been white without any Creole in the mix, then little Daphne might have said well hello to somewhere a whole lot different than a shack in old Louisiana.

You get to my age, man, and you think about these things. Why we live the lives we do. My mother, rest in peace, used to say the good Lord decides but I don't go with that because if he did and he was a true Lord like Ma said then he wouldn't have come up with the idea of white folks. My woman back home says the Lord just had a bad day on that particular occasion but you could say the same thing about coward Bob Ford and nobody forgives him. If someone knows what happened to Daphne after the trumpet player met his maker, they sure ain't told me. It wasn't like the killing of Frank was in all the LA papers. I know what I know from folks talking. You hear things from folks, but some things you don't hear. Well, you can't hear everything. As my dear mother, rest in peace, used to say, there ain't enough hours in the day to know what happens to folks. People pass you by in this life. I was told that Daphne had earned a living working with the guys Frank knew. She didn't mind black folks, which is no surprise considering how she was fixed with relatives, so she could have, I figure. Maybe she was good with the books and records and did something like that. From what I heard Frank was no bookkeeper.

Yes, sir, I know Easy Rawlins. I can't say I ever took to the man.

Easy was always up to something, and it was hard to relax when he was around. But he stuck by his friend Mouse who was definitely no knife man because he shot too many people, so I'll give Easy credit for that. It took him a few years but Easy got his detective licence. I know the police liked the work Easy did that one time to stop the man that was killing the black girls. No Black Dahlia killer roaming these streets, all thanks to Easy. No, sir, Easy had it figured. And I can't say Easy wasn't straight with me because he was. Easy always told you up front what he was going to do next. What Easy did wasn't wrong. The guy had property, and I don't blame him for wanting to own his house and live in a suburb just like white folks. But when he bought buildings and then rented them out to black families I didn't feel the same about old Easy. And I don't care what rent he charged. Easy didn't turn away from his own but he had to have more than the rest of us. I heard he was good with children, and his two kids did just fine although none of the ladies in the life of Easy Rawlins stayed around for long. Easy adopted a daughter, which a lot of men wouldn't, but just like white folks he had to send her to some stuck up private school. So it was no surprise to hear that something loving had happened between Easy and Daphne. He was always watching how white folks lived. The joke is that the next of kin to Daphne was as black as me.

Okay, Easy may have done right with his kind, and more than once, but I just didn't like him wanting what he wanted. You understand me? I'll talk true. When I heard that Frank 'The Knife' had been ready to slice the throat of Easy and would have done just that if Mouse hadn't put a pistol to the head of Frank, well, I imagined Frank and Easy without Mouse in the room. Inside my head I saw Easy dead on the floor just like Jesse James after coward Rob Ford did what he did. I think to myself, if that had happened, would I be heartbroken. No, sir, I don't reckon I would.

JOE GILLIS

SUNSET BOULEVARD
USA 1950
DIRECTOR – BILLY WILDER

You want a drink? Have a drink. You're young. Enjoy it while you can. Let my secretary get you a cold beer. Janet, get the guy a drink and tell Betty I need a yes or no today on that Western script. No, Janet, I don't want a beer, doctor's orders. Son, my stomach gives me hell. Of course I don't mind you writing a book about what happened between Norma Desmond and Joe Gillis, long as you don't want me to make a film of the sorry saga. That would soon have them heading for the exits. You know, people say what happened between Joe and Norma must have damaged the studio and that was why we moved so quickly into television but it didn't and it wasn't. Despite what she thought, Norma Desmond had already been forgotten by our great cinema going public. And by the time our publicity man had finished, well, Joe Gillis had not even worked here which was kind of half true because the guy never had a screen credit. One of his ideas might have been borrowed by someone somewhere sometime but no more than that.

Here's your drink. Taste okay? Good, you can have a real drink. No, okay, stick to the beer. Thanks for the beer, Janet. No, I wasn't shocked by what happened between Joe and Norma. There was a difference between their ages. So what? Think this through, my friend. This town has more young beautiful women than I've seen anywhere. And I don't mean like Paris. These women here in Los Angeles are built. How many young beauties have I seen draped over the arm of some old well-dressed guy who believes his wardrobe and weekly haircut and manicure make him irresistible? I've lost count. I lose count in a day. Not that I keep track any more.

Money, power and sex, it happens. Maybe it shouldn't but it does. Look at that thing with Liz Short, the Black Dahlia girl. It was all over the papers a couple of years back. I saw Liz at parties, saw old men crawling over this beautiful woman and her just grinning as if they were doing her a favour. Liz Short finished up dead and almost cut in half. We all got a memo. Stay away from the funeral. Mark Hansen threw sleazy parties in his palace on Carlos Avenue. The same piece of slime groomed Hollywood wannabes for careers in cheap, sixteen millimetre, black and white nudie movies.

Joe Gillis was like the women I see every day. He was looking for a way into the movie business. More than a few mentioned him dying in the swimming pool, as if only they were the ones that understood irony. I don't see many dead bodies floating on the surface of swimming pools but I see plenty of people like Joe Gillis around the pools and believe me they look great in bikinis. Norma had been a big star and she had money but she was lonely. I can see why the woman thought she was entitled. Beer taste okay? Good, you don't have to sip it. I have a fridge full of them out there. You know, us talking like this has me thinking. Not once have I ever wondered if Janet has sneaked a beer. Why's that you think? Maybe, I'm not sure what a beer drinker looks like.

Betty Schaefer was there on Sunset Boulevard the night Norma killed Joe. Betty still works for me as a reader and she's still dreaming about being a writer. I tell her she is a kind of writer because the scripts won't be the same after she's read them. I just don't let Betty anywhere near a typewriter. Betty was distraught after what happened to Joe. I can sort of understand how she feels. Sort of because, unlike Betty, I've never kissed someone that later has been plugged in the back. There's a couple I've felt like plugging but that's another story. Betty rated Joe but whether she would have done if he'd had no hair like me, I don't know. I liked the man. All he ever wanted was to be a writer, not even rich or famous, and, well, I'm a softie for that kind of ambition. Don't grin at me. I'm not ashamed of having a tender heart. It helps me relax at night.

JOE GILLIS

Not enough but it helps.

Betty and Joe worked together on a script. No, it was never filmed. The thing had its moments but I couldn't work it out. And if old Sheldrake is missing the point then I can assure you our great cinema audience won't find it either. I was at the preview of the Welles' picture. That's the one, The Magnificent Ambersons. I'll never forget that night. It wasn't even my picture, and I wanted to fall down into the ground. As I say to Betty every day, don't even think about masterpieces. The truth is that Betty liked Joe Gillis. After her thing with Joe she took a break from her husband-to-be Artie Green which I kind of understand because I never took to Artie. Understand me, I see a lot of ambition. Even sweet Betty Schaefer two rooms down the corridor has ambition. But when that ambition is mixed with innocent eager enthusiasm, then it doesn't work for me. I want writers and movie makers to see the world as it is. Artie Green was enthusiastic about everybody. You get me? That's what I liked about Joe. He had the ambition but not that back slapping enthusiasm which just makes my stomach ache more than it does already.

Look, try and understand this. I have this friend, an ex-policeman here in Los Angeles. He decided he wanted to be a writer and, guess what, the man hits pay dirt. This was back when we were sparing with the four letter words. Well, these books by this cop were not. Critics said the public responded to the realism of life on the streets. Me, I think the American public just wanted to read a book with a lot of four letter words. What am I trying to say? I've forgotten. Oh yes, this policeman said something to me one night. We were eating some Mexican thing in this out of town place. The cop thought it was wonderful. Me, it just made my stomach ache. This cop said that in his job he didn't see the worst people but just people at their worst.

George, I said, that was his name, George, you should work in Hollywood.

Look, think this through. Joe Gillis was offered a good deal.

Norma was paying him five hundred dollars a week, he was living in a swanky place and he was doing what he wanted to do. He was writing a script. Okay he had to bang a dame that wouldn't see fifty again but, you know, those old silent movie stars had to climb the same pole that starlets do today. Norma would have known a few bedroom tricks, I'm certain. One of these days I'll tell you all about Mabel Norman and how she had fun. My God, what a woman. I know, that's another book.

I know, I know. Betty has told me more than once about Joe having a sense of honour, how honourable Joe didn't worry about not having his name on the script that they worked on together. Certainly, I know that Joe told Betty she could have the script as a present. And Joe was even loyal to Artie. Sweet little Betty made the first move, not Joe. And when Joe walked out on Norma, or tried to, he made sure first that Betty went back to Artie, our favourite back slapper. You're looking at me as if I'm talking bull. I know what you're going to say. How could a guy who knew how to do right sell himself to a woman twice his age?

You really want to understand? Stay in that chair and watch me work for a week. What did that cop who wrote all the four letter words say? In his job he saw the worst in people. And so do I, believe me. People will do anything to be in the movies. Those beautiful women I mentioned. Not only do they offer treats they shouldn't, the men they're giving the treats to don't have a problem with promising me the same women. And I'm not just talking about the well paid ladies for the weekend. Men have offered me their wives if I could get them a part. No, you're wrong, it's not just the hopefuls. I've had big time directors in here pleading for favours and promising what I'd rather not remember, big names that would shock you. Oh, but Sheldrake, I have to have so and so photograph the picture, or edit it, or add the music. One guy said he'd commit suicide if I didn't get the guy on his last picture that had done the noise of the horses galloping. You want to hear the noise a horse makes? See, I can do it with a glass on a desk.

JOE GILLIS

Look, when you work in a business that preaches what you do is more important than life or death, then you are going to see people, as the cop said, at their worst. And we now have these French critics analysing our movies from here in Hollywood as if they offer moral guidance. Give me a break. It doesn't add up. Do you think it adds up? Sometimes, what kind of answer is that? Sometimes, well, maybe you're right. Sometimes is how it added up for poor Joe Gillis and Norma Desmond. Don't say anything but I'm not sure it's adding up for Betty Schaefer and Artie Green. What did Oscar Wilde say? We can resist everything but temptation. Joe Gillis was an all right guy until he had the opportunity to be not all right. You know, I said before it was made that The Picture of Dorian Gray would be a turkey. Dr Jekyll and Mr Hyde, now that was a good movie and popular, too. That book wasn't by Oscar Wilde? I didn't know that. I always thought. I do get those old English guys confused.

MICKEY COHEN

GANGSTER SQUAD
USA 2013
DIRECTOR – RUBIN FLEISCHER

Living with Mickey wasn't so hard. Honey, I've known worse. The truth is I've always been a flirt. I notice men and I like it when they smile at me. Some women give the come on because they like guys hanging from their elbows. They want the power, you understand me? I'm not like that. I have a sweet nature. Mickey told me so. With me, a nice smile from friendly eyes and my guard drops. Every time? Almost every time. And Jerry had one of the cutest grins in LA. Remember Jerry? He was one of LAPD's finest, so fine they dragged him into the Gangster Squad. But like Mickey, there was a rough side to Jerry Wooters.

Imagine, I'm living with Mickey Cohen and seeing this LA detective in hotels over all LA. I regret nothing, baby. Jerry was the same guy who put the bug in the very house where I was living with Mickey. I even bumped into him when he was doing it. Jerry insisted there was just the one bug in the TV, so at least I didn't have Jerry listening to me and Mickey when we were, you know. So Jerry said, but Jerry had an answer for everything.

Mickey found this young tutor to help him with his reading and writing and other stuff. I never had a teacher that looked like this guy. Lou had such sweet eyes, not like Jerry but he was a swell kid, straight out of college. Son of one of the guys that Mickey knew but nothing like his old man.

When I walked in on the lessons, Lou, this kid, would switch on like a light bulb. So every time Mickey had Lou round I would make it a policy to go in and grin. It sure put a smile on the face of this Lou. It would annoy Mickey but that didn't bother me one bit.

Every time Mickey would say the same thing, Grace, I'm trying to concentrate. And then he would look at Lou giving him lessons and say, We're both trying to concentrate, ain't we teacher?

Well, Lou would go pink and lower his head and start reading whatever book he had on his lap. And if Mickey weren't looking, I would give Lou a wink.

And then I would say, Mickey, it ain't my fault you never went to school as a kid like the rest of us.

And then Mickey would say, If I had, doll, you wouldn't be living in this palace like the Queen of Sheba.

And then, every time Mickey would look at the kid next to him and say, Somerset Maugham, eh Lou.

And then Lou would say, Somerset Maugham, Mr Cohen.

After that I had to listen to them chuckle and I would walk out the room. But the next week when Lou came back with his books I would still walk in, and every time, well, you know already.

And the Somerset Maugham guy? Jerry went to the library and found me this book. And as soon as I read the first story, I got wise. In this story there's a gravedigger. He works for the local church somewhere in England, and the church has to get modern and have proper accounts. And this means the gravedigger now has to sign for his wages. Only problem is the gravedigger can't read or write. So they give this gravedigger the heave ho but him and his lady have lived cheap and they've got some cash stacked and they open a shop. This is okay because the wife can read and write. A lucky break, yeah? The shop does well, and the guy and his wife open more and then a chain right across England. The gravedigger and his dame are in clover, not like Mickey maybe, but loaded, yeah. With all this cash the gravedigger makes a will. Of course, he has to sign the papers with some lawyer. And the gravedigger says no thanks he can't read nor write. The lawyer is shocked because this guy on the other side of the desk is really loaded.

He says, You've accumulated all this wealth. Imagine what you could have been if you'd been able to read and write.

That's easy, says the now rich man. I'd have been a gravedigger.

Funny, eh. It made me chuckle. Before Lou came along, Mickey couldn't read or write which is why Mickey and Lou talked about this Somerset Maugham. Mickey couldn't even count. He knew which dollar bills were worth more than the others but that was about it. He'd put them in different piles, fifties, twenties, tens and so on. Mickey knew the difference between little piles and tall piles and that was about it. But after Lou and a few others showing him what was what Mickey was different. After that Mickey could read and write, add, subtract and even multiply and divide. And in the end he writes this book, an autobiography. Of course, he had help but, when it was finished, he read it which was something, I guess.

Baby, I took the stand against Mickey because I had to but I wouldn't have if there'd been no Detective Sergeant Jerry Wooters whispering in my ear. And what happens? Mickey only walks free because running his trial is the one judge that's in his pocket.

The Gangster Squad in LA claim all sorts but why does Mickey go inside? Not because of some Gangster Squad. Tax evasion is why. And why? Because Mickey Cohen just had to be in the limelight. And that meant going to the piles of dollar bills. The witnesses that hurt Mickey were not folks like me who wanted to talk about Mickey pulling the trigger on someone. No, just a bunch of shopkeepers and accountants which makes sense because Mickey never did make a go of going legit.

It don't square how Mickey liked seeing his name in the papers so much because the same guy was at his happiest on the back lawn messing with his dogs. You heard about the special bed he made for Tuffy? The thing was an exact replica of the bed Mickey and me slept in. Not the same size, of course, but creepy, yes. Mickey and me in one big fancy bed, and right there on the floor next to us is little Tuffy sleeping in his bed that looks just the same. Mickey cried at his funeral. Tuffy was buried with the best, next to the dogs and cats of movie stars.

One hundred times a day is an exaggeration but it was a lot.

Mickey was always washing his hands. Now if you said fifty a day, baby, I might be tempted to say yes. Not that I ever kept count. I remember him having showers that lasted a couple of hours. He was particular, I suppose. Everything had to be just so. Mickey is the only man I ever lived with whose wardrobe was bigger than mine. And one thing I can say is true. He never wore the same suit more than once. The same with everything.

Bugsy and Capone were dressers and chatty with it. Personally, I think that was the problem Mickey had. He didn't know whether he wanted to be Bugsy Siegel or Al Capone and so he copied them both. The newsboys said he was trying to move up in the world. I ain't gonna say that ain't true but what Mickey really wanted was to walk in a room like Bugsy could. Capone I never saw. Bugsy, I did, and I ain't ashamed to say I'll never forget it. Mickey was complicated. I was already passed over when he got into that Christianity stuff with Billy Graham whose preaching was as big back then as it is now. I believe what I heard, that Mickey thought being a Christian might give him a better way of life. But Mickey just had to spend money and be noticed, and his damned haberdashery was never going to give him the money Mickey needed. If his book had hit bigger and they'd made a movie like he wanted with Mickey as Mickey, it might have been different. The movie stars he had done favours for were no help but then those people have their own problems. The movie didn't happen, and Mickey went back to the rackets. Maybe he was different second time around.

I didn't count the number of times Mickey washed his hands and I know nothing about the number of people he rubbed out except they were a lot and that he started early. And Detective Sergeant Wooters? Cute smiles don't last forever, baby. The last time I met him he bought me a swell meal and smiled a lot but all he wanted to talk about was the Black Dahlia killing and how him and three of his pals from the Gangster Squad went to this motel to hear about some woman who disappeared and left a lot of blood behind.

Jerry said him and his mates on the Gangster Squad were about to nail the guy that did the murder. And then, typical LAPD, the Gangster Squad boys were pulled off the case. No explanation, said Jerry, except his language was a lot stronger than mine. Jerry quit the cops after that but it made no difference to me and him.

We could have nailed her killer, said Jerry.

But there was this guy with three names that had connections according to Jerry and somehow he was involved. And it took a lot of effort to shut Jerry up about the Black Dahlia killing. I should have listened more. If I'd got some names, maybe I could have written a book like Mickey. Jerry also mentioned this guy with a big Adam's Apple, a Norwegian guy, I think. But really? I was trying to enjoy my swanky meal. One thing I will say about Mickey. I never heard him swear in front of women.

DIXON STEELE

IN A LONELY PLACE
USA 1950
DIRECTOR – NICHOLAS RAY

You're asking me if I can talk about Dixon Steele? I'm Mel Lippman. I was an almost famous Hollywood agent. Actually I was famous although it never felt like that. I made telephone calls, met people, attended meetings and pitched for my writers. All day and every day I did nothing but talk. I talked and talked and I'm talking now. Listen, Dixon Steele had talent but he was never the same man after the war. The man that came back from the unholy scrap with Japan was different and, I have to say, he had a much expanded notion of his own importance. What he missed about the war was the heroism. That's my opinion.

The movie scripts of Dixon Steele were always quality, right until the end. But tastes change, and after the war Dix took himself a little more seriously. He was more than intolerant. He was antagonistic. Dix was paid to turn books into film scripts but our hero was more interested in the stories he wanted to tell which meant that the scripts Dix produced were nothing like the books he was given to work on. Somehow, though, he always made a living. He lived in West Hollywood, in a fine old Spanish style building that had gorgeous pink walls. The tall palm trees outside had these large bright green leaves that brushed against the red stone tiles of the sloping roofs. I know. I should have been a writer, though maybe not.

People were wary of Dix but he was liked. On a good night in his company there was nowhere else in the world you would rather be. Some said he was moody but it was more how he reacted to moments. The man did not like his authority to be challenged.

After being a captain in the war he felt entitled to give orders. Dix was not the only writer that liked to lash out or drink more than he should. That was the tradition back then. But most writers settled for caustic wit and they were at least predictable. You felt the lash of their tongues and learned what not to say. Dix was as caustic as the rest but on a bad night he would explode and someone might have to go to hospital. Fortunately he worked in Hollywood, and the next day after the best medical treatment it would be forgotten.

The '50s in Hollywood were not good. It's a coincidence but as television became popular Dixon Steele ran out of movie hits. We all suffered a little but Dix also had a war to remember. The business with Mildred Dickinson, though, was bad. And none of that would have happened if Dix had done what he was paid to do which was to sit down with the damned book and read it. Instead, Dix had to pick up Mildred and take her home so she could tell him all about the book. I blame myself. I lent Mildred the book. I had no idea she would read it, a hat check girl. Don't ask me the title of the book. After what happened I refuse to mention it. The movie was a hit, though. Lousy but a hit, like the book.

On her way home from where Dix lived poor Mildred Atkinson was killed, thrown out of a car and on to the freeway. I always had a feeling that the cops would have liked the killer to be the guy that was responsible for the Black Dahlia killing. Everyone knew that Bill Parker the LAPD Commissioner had a thirst for publicity. Something must have put those cops in a bad mood because they went after Dix. That was a bad time for Dix. He had the war to think about and he was a murder suspect. I keep mentioning the war. He knew he was innocent, and so did I. I'll be honest. A couple of times I had doubts. Dix had murdered Japs in the war, there I go again, and he was always ready for a fight. If he hadn't been capable of killing then the police wouldn't have got to him and Laurel. But violence, contempt and hatred for others Dixon Steele had in spades.

He used to say to me, Mel, folks are as awful as me. I don't like myself and I sure as hell don't like the rest.

Among screenwriters, of course, this is not a feeling unique to Dixon Steele.

I liked Laurel although I was as nervous of Laurel Gray as I was wary of Dixon Steele. That masseuse she had in tow gave me the creeps. Laurel went to New York after she finished with Dix. I drove Laurel to the airport but the damned masseuse was on the back seat all the way talking about how the last thing sweet Laurel needed was another man in her life. This masseuse was not a lady you wanted to meet on a dark night. There was a European writer whose name I can't remember. He wanted to write a script for a Wagner opera type movie. Can you imagine? There was a rumour that Sam Goldwyn thought about the idea for at least ten minutes. If they ever do make a movie of The Ring, this masseuse will be the first name on the cast list. I can guarantee.

Laurel had an apartment in the building where Dix lived. They met in the courtyard the same night Dix was saying goodbye to Mildred. The courtyard was a pleasant place to sit. It had shrubs and potted cactus plants and an art deco fountain. I liked going to those apartments. Not that I had much choice. I had to hang around. Worrying about Dixon Steele and deadlines was how I earned my salary.

We were all restless that autumn in 1950. I remember there being a monster of a Santa Ana wind. Those things are so humid they exhaust you. The Santa Ana and the murder of Mildred made everyone edgy. And for Dix that meant him lashing out at whoever was in reach. One way he got things out of his system was driving like a maniac. The hero complex again, you see. No, I'm not going to mention where he got it. Dix had more than one stand-up row with other drivers. One ended with Dix slugging this gridiron guy. Laurel was in the car and saw everything. After that particular incident Laurel not only doubted Dix as a potential husband but she also suspected that maybe he really had choked Mildred to death and thrown her out on the freeway. Laurel became cold to Dix. There were no more shared dishes of guacamole and glasses of white wine after that. And the last thing a girl should do if Dixon Steele is in love with her is ease off on the emotions. Dixon can smell mistrust a mile off. I suppose he sharpened the instinct in the war. I know, I've mentioned it again.

Everybody asks me what happened to Dixon Steele after Laurel headed out to New York. He was distraught, especially so because Dix knew he was to blame. But as time passed Dix told himself things would have been different if poor Mildred had not been killed. And by her boyfriend would you believe. A good looking guy, too. Knowing that helped, and after the damned Santa Ana wind blew away everyone settled.

The cops gave Dix a rough ride but even without the cops Dix and Laurel wouldn't have lasted. At some point Dix would have forgotten himself and Laurel would have headed for the exit. The last I heard Laurel was living with the damned masseuse. Do I think Laurel was bisexual? There had to be something about that Valkyrie that interested Laurel.

Dixon Steele lasted another four years in Hollywood. None of his other scripts made the big time, and nobody expected that they would. Dix was a reduced proposition, and one of my meal tickets was clipped.

I did what I could. I brought in a private eye to help Dix stay focussed and to keep him out of fights. The private eye was called Marlowe and he had a way with words that not only stopped the fights but Dix liked. The problem was that Dix and Marlowe would spend most of the day drinking bourbon and discussing what was wrong with the world and Los Angeles. Marlowe left because he knew he was drinking too much, and I brought in another guy called Jake Gittes. Not a success, I'm afraid. Gittes was as capable of starting fights as Dix. The inevitable happened. They slung punches at one another, an argument about Noah Cross or someone. It was a shame because Dix liked private eyes.

He once went up to Bridgeport to research this thing where a private eye called Markham was supposed to have killed four people. Dix came up with a script but by then no one was watching movies about private eyes. I told Dix we should try television, and we did but it came to nothing.

I never saw Dix again after he went over to Ireland to polish some script about the Republican Army. That was the last work he ever did for Hollywood. Dix liked Ireland. He said it soothed him. Dix settled in the village where Ford had filmed The Quiet Man with Duke Wayne. From the little I know Dix kept out of fights. Dix stopped drinking bourbon, switched to Guinness and became fat but nothing like the masseuse that had the hold over Laurel. I expected him to find a nice Irish girl but he never did. I wonder if it was something about the Irish brogue that stopped Dix looking for fights. Or maybe he just got old like the rest of us. I heard he wrote a couple of scripts for BBC television. I hope they appreciated him. The man could write. I was just pleased he had taken his typewriter.

MAL GRAINGER

711 OCEAN DRIVE
USA 1950
DIRECTOR – JOSEPH M NEWMAN

Mal always had a plan. He certainly had a plan for little old me, Gail Mason. The first time Mal looked at me something registered in his eyes. No doubt desire was in there but you could see right from the beginning, even before Mal held you in his arms, that this was a man making a plan, calculating the next steps. That was why Mal Grainger liked money so much, why he took it so seriously. Money gave his brain something to count. Trudy Maxwell was the accountant that Mal used to help him run his wire service. I really liked Trudy and for a while I felt bad about her because I thought Mal had thrown Trudy over for me. But then I met Trudy and realised she was the one that had said farewell to Mal. But for a while Mal played around with Trudy, and she will tell you the same as me. The first time he looked into her eyes she knew he had a plan and it made her curious. Some men are like that, somehow you believe what is behind their eyes. Mal didn't have the prettiest eyes. You know what I was thinking when we were trying to escape from the police across the Boulder Dam? Why am I doing all this with a guy that I know will go fat and isn't even handsome? The truth is that Mal Grainger had eyes that made promises.

Darling, there is not a man I've known that at some point I wished I hadn't met. If I'd been different, had a less affluent family, perhaps I'd have met some decent man with not that much money in his pocket but a heart of gold. But I grew up surrounded by money and the men responsible for that money. The only advice I had came from wives that had rich husbands. In that world you don't have as many options as people think. Lieutenant, you need to interrupt more. I'm beginning to sound as if I feel sorry for myself.

Maybe that was why I indulged Mal. Alright, why I found him attractive. He looked like someone whose eyes couldn't lie. And the truth is that most of the time his eyes didn't although Mal did string me along for a while after he had Larry killed. Larry was my husband, and, if I were not sitting here facing two detectives because of that plan Mal had, I would say Larry was the biggest mistake in my life. I did lose some enthusiasm for Mal after Larry was killed but Larry had raised his fists to me. I know that seeing me bruised and lying in a hospital bed had upset Mal although I was also aware that Mal was sore about the money the syndicate was skimming off the wire service that he operated. And by then Mal and me needed one another. I told myself that if we could get away from Los Angeles and Vegas it would be different. The problem was that Mal came up with a plan to take back some of the money the syndicate had robbed from his wire service. Mal Grainger died because he had one plan too many although we must not forget the contribution of our fine trigger happy policemen.

We already had two hundred and fifty thousand dollars, and that was enough for any pair of sweethearts to start a new life, even if one of those sweethearts had my background. I told Mal that in Guatemala, which was where Mal decided we should live, we could get by on that kind of money forever. Chippie, who was this sweet little man who brought Mal into the wire service, said the same. Mal thought differently. What happened to Chippie. The syndicate is what happened to Chippie. No one sees Chippie around anymore because he isn't around. I'm afraid, darling, it's as simple as that.

The syndicate is what happened to us all. Carl Stephans was as smooth and as sinister as the men I knew back home. No, dear, his name is not Carl Stephens. It's Stephans. His parents were South African but Carl sounded more English than anything. He claimed he was connected to really important people back in South Africa which was probably why he sounded so English. Charming or not,

Carl Stephans had people killed. I can't say I heard him say murder this man or that man. I do know certain people disappeared. Perhaps I could identify some faces from your files. I've always been good with faces. Not so good with eyes but good with faces.

I'm afraid, dear, that I don't know that much but I do know that Stephans took over the business that Mal ran. Carl already had a business that stretched from back east to Kansas but he wanted to run a coast to coast wire service. Lieutenant, none of these men can be criticised for a lack of ambition. Indeed, Carl Stephans had a really big plan. That's the problem with men. Too many men have plans but, darling, I wouldn't like a man without one.

Not all the syndicate men had the best table manners but I am glad to say that, whatever faults Larry had, he didn't embarrass you at the dinner table. Larry did struggle with sentences which was why he could be dull company. Carl Stephans was different. He had an opinion about everything and he was charming. I'm sorry, darling. Is this boring you? I am cooperating. Of course I've realised I aided and abetted a murderer but I didn't know that at the time. I'm truly sorry Mal set up the trick with the phones to deceive you, Lieutenant. I didn't know his plan was to convince you that he wasn't here in LA and he was making his call from Palm Springs. And I had no idea that Mal had committed a murder. I just assumed he was in trouble over the wire service. He was the man in my life, and I helped him. I didn't even know what I was doing. I put two telephones next to an amplifier. It was all too technical for me, dear. No, I haven't been talking to my lawyer. I am cooperating. Being cooperative is in my nature.

You mean in the sense that sweet Trudy worked, performed tasks and had a boss that pays you a salary? No, women from families like mine don't do that kind of thing. I collect rich men and drink more than I should. No, I'm not proud of myself. Men or money, I'm not sure who or which makes the biggest promises or tells the biggest lies. I never told lies to Mal and I doubt Trudy did either. Mal was lucky that way because there are plenty of men and women out there telling lies to each other every day. Mal was unlucky because he believed money could solve all your troubles. Chippie knew Mal when he worked for the telephone company. Chippie said Mal was likeable back then. Mal used to give some of his money to the guys who had families to raise. Not much but something. Chippie said that Mal never took a full wage packet home. When I heard the story I thought how sweet. But even back then Mal thought the solution to everything was money. Once the wire service was making huge profits Mal became mean with his money. Trudy warned him but Mal had to raise the price of his wire service. Some of the bookmakers that used his wire service went bankrupt but that was of no concern to Mal. That was the point when I should have walked away from Mal but I didn't. There was an exception, this deaf and dumb guy that used to fix one of his cars. Mal lent him a couple of thousand so that the deaf and dumb guy could put the money away and set up a business and work with honest people for a change. This dumb and deaf guy had owned a garage in this small town called Bridgeport and it was his dream to buy it back and return to the quiet life in the Rockies.

To be honest what happens with the wire service baffles me. Of course, darling, I know how it operates. The company running the wire service owns the equipment that delivers the results to the bookmakers and sends it over the wire quick enough to stop punters that know the winners putting bets on before the bookies have received the result. But even though Mal explained it all to me, stuff about transmitters, telephones and the rest, I still don't know what equipment they used and how it works. But what baffled me more was how people like Mal and Carl Stephans made so much money from just running a wire service. There are that many bookmakers in California? I didn't know that. Carl, of course, had the coast to coast operation. He was really rich. Mal said that the wire service was legitimate, that there was nothing illegal about passing information on from the racetracks. It doesn't seem right, something legal being run by gangsters.

Yes, of course, there is the money. It explains so much, doesn't it, darling? But if the wire service is an honest business, why haven't honest businessmen come along and provided an alternative wire service? Lieutenant, I understand people like Carl Stephans know how to intimidate competitors but there are ruthless men running rich and powerful companies in this country. I suppose you're right. These people do talk to one another and they will concoct their plans. Meanwhile the poor scrimp and scheme. And call me stupid but if people can bet at the racetracks why not let them bet with a bookmaker? What's the difference? No, I don't suppose that will ever happen. Ah, my lawyer has arrived. Thank you, Lieutenant, thank you for opening the door. A lady likes a courteous man. Who are those two old people waiting by the desk? They haven't done anything wrong, I hope. They're the parents of Mal. Oh dear, I didn't expect that they would look so poor.

WEBB GARWOOD

THE PROWLER
USA 1951
DIRECTOR – JOSEPH LOSEY

I don't want to count the years Bud and me have been married. There are a lot of them. I don't regret any. I'm serious. Some of my friends have remarked about how Bud always introduces me as the war department. That doesn't bother me. I'm well used to it, and I never did like the name Grace anyhow. Bud Crocker is a good man and a fine policeman. All those years doing that job and wandering across the streets of LA he has never thrown a punch or shot at anyone. He says that to me. And I reckon he can count the number of times on one hand he has raised his voice to folks.

We have to remember. Webb Garwood was a good policeman before it all went wrong, before he met lonely Susan Gilvray and saw her beautiful big house. Sure, Webb hated the job and moaned about being nothing more than a dumb cop but he worked hard. Bud said that Webb, having no family and everything, was always willing to do that little extra to make life easier for Bud. Most nights Webb dropped Bud off outside our door. Webb parked the cop car in the station while Bud was at home with me. I liked Webb for that.

But I never no way took to Webb Garwood the man. I disliked how Webb would pretend to listen when Bud was talking about his rock collection. Okay, Bud can go on and on about the rocks he's picked up over the years but Webb could have said something once in a while. Webb was happy enough to eat our food and drink Bud's beer. The truth is that Webb Garwood made me uneasy. Talk to the man face to face and you thought he was talking to the best friend he ever had. But watch Webb talk to someone else, as I did when Bud showed off his precious rocks, and you saw something cold. Still, I can see how he charmed Susan Gilvray. I have often imagined them talking face to face and Susan melting like a fool. I met Susan a few times. I went to the inquest after Webb shot her husband and I was a guest when Webb and Susan married. She was a looker, and when Bud said she had some figure I knew it was best to keep quiet. But I could tell right away. Susan was a poor wounded creature and had been well before she met Webb Garwood. I said the same to Bud but he scoffed. All Bud saw were the killer eyes and the luscious figure.

Girls who look like that, don't get pushed around, Bud said to me.

I told him that it's the babes that get used by men more than the homely women. Bud went back to reading his paper.

We both saw Webb get shot by the police out in Calico. He struggled up this rocky slope but he was finished well before he got to the top of the hill and well before the bullets slapped into his back and killed him stone dead. Sorry, I don't mean to be crude. Something like that, though, stays with you. Bud and me never did go back to Calico after that. We were making a visit to surprise Webb and Susan. Bud had told Webb about Calico when he was going on about his rocks, so Webb must have been listening after all. Bud and me took Susan to the nearest hospital. The cops led the way but everyone thought she'd be more relaxed with Bud and me.

Susan Gilvray never did return to LA. We still get a Christmas card every year from Susan. I send her one each year, too. I always say the same thing. Stay away from the men, honey, they are trouble. Bud is fine but life is quiet and that takes two. I can live with quiet, and Bud having no ambition was no concern to me. Bud was security but there is a price to pay for everything. In a marriage you have to recognise that it's not just you paying the price. Susan was not the kind of girl that could understand that. If she had, she may have settled with her rich husband and not been tempted by Webb.

Men did bad things to Susan, I know that. You may not remember but there was a big scandal in LA police a couple of years after the thing with Webb. They closed down this call girl business, Fleur-de-Lis or something. It was all over the papers, and anyone who was a policeman had to help. Bud was asked by the detectives to do a search of some big house that the girls all used but as well as that they went through the homes of the Hollywood customers. Susan was no hooker but in more than one of these houses belonging to movie stars and film producers Bud found various sex photos. Susan was in there. She wasn't just naked. Bud said what he saw Susan doing was degrading. You can imagine, and I don't want to talk about it, a beautiful girl like that. Bud brought the photographs of Susan home and set fire to them. I worried about his job and what might happen if someone found out but Bud said there was enough filth to keep the LA police department busy for a year and that nothing ever happened to the Hollywood big shots anyway. Bud hasn't taken me to a cinema to watch a movie since then. Still, we get around the country looking for rocks. These days Bud is less interested in rocks than the mountains. We've found a lovely spot near this small town, Bridgeport, mountains and a beautiful lake. Nothing much happens in Bridgeport which is a fine place although they did a few years back have some big story about this private eye that went around killing people.

I asked Susan just what it was that she saw in Webb Garwood.

I loved him so much I was afraid of him, she said.

I suppose Susan realised she wanted the excitement but there was always a cost. I'm not excusing men, and neither does my husband Bud Crocker, especially after that big Fleur-de Lis case. But, as soon as I saw Susan, I knew there was something wrong, and it wasn't just damage. You could see it in her eyes. There was a tiredness, a weariness there, a big loneliness in the middle of her heart. The poor kid hoped that men would be the answer. But, instead of falling for those promises, what Susan should have done was taken that cold brick in her heart and kept it solid, polished it like a diamond. That way she could have survived and avoided Webb Garwood. Bud can polish a rock so it looks like a diamond.

Bud says that Webb was no natural killer. Bud just thinks that Webb and Susan weren't right for one another. Yet they had something in common. They were two people who both thought they were no good. The difference was Susan hated herself but Webb thought everyone was like him. Webb hated the world although no one guessed he was like that until the news came out. I suppose you have to hate the world a little if you're going to pull the trigger on a man who has done you no harm. But, as I said, face to face Webb Garwood was charming. The man had dangerous dreams, and the husband of Susan was in the way. What surprised me most was Webb shooting himself in the arm to make it look like an accident. Webb was smart and not lazy.

Bud used to say to him, I get it, Webb, you have ambition but there are places in the force for folks that want careers.

Most cops who want the extra dollars would have settled for becoming a detective. I know Webb got a place in college but he fell out with the basketball coach. So Webb could have had a real career in the police. That Captain who was killed and all the papers said died a hero wanted Webb as a detective. Captain Dudley Smith saw something in Webb Garwood that he thought could be used. Like Susan, I suppose, Dudley Smith fell for the promises of Webb except Webb never did become a detective.

The big question is did Webb Garwood love Susan Gilvray. They came from the same small town and, as I said, that was not all they had in common. They looked happy enough when I saw them together. I really do believe they felt desire for each other. Something happened to them when they were in each other's arms. Webb and Susan also wanted what went with each other. Susan had the money Webb needed for the motel that he had always wanted to buy, and Webb was young and exciting and scared Susan a little. Some women need to be scared. I said that to Bud when he was shaking his head about the photographs he'd seen of Susan, the poor kid. Bud and me saw the motel that Webb bought with Susan's money. Webb took Susan out to Calico so that Susan would have their baby in secret. We worked out where they'd be after we called unannounced at their fancy motel. Webb was frightened the police would nail him as the suspect for the murder of her husband when they discovered she was not long pregnant after her husband died. Susan was close to giving birth when they went to the hideaway in Calico that Bud had mentioned. If Susan had got pregnant a few months later, would Susan and Webb have settled down to a happy married life? They looked as if they were in love when they went off after their marriage. They could have been happy together. Of course, Susan wouldn't have known that she was living with a murderer. Webb liked money, though, and I reckon he would have always wanted more. But I am not called the war department by Bud for nothing. I can think the worst of people. Maybe that is why I picked a man who was more interested in collecting rocks than banknotes.

CAPTAIN DUDLEY LIAM SMITH

LA CONFIDENTIAL
USA 1997
DIRECTOR – CURTIS HANSON

The Christmas Eve it all happened, I was a forty-two year old low grade hack. I wrote fodder to fill those middle of the newspaper pages that most readers never reached. I was also going bald. I had taken along a photographer to the police station but all we expected was a posed photo of a couple of grinning and worse for wear detectives. Joe the photographer had the same zilch career prospects as me. We were a pair of nobodies with families we were not feeding very well. The big boys on the paper were at home with their loved ones.

We all know what happened. Down in the cells there was this unholy scrap between the cops and these Mexican guys. The cops were all liquored up, and I still have no idea how no one was killed. All Joe the photographer could see was arms in the air and fists being thrown but, like a trooper, he held his camera high and snapped as often as he could. People ask me how many photos Joe took amidst the chaos. He took four which was no small achievement considering he had to keep changing the flash bulbs while being knocked side to side by crazy coppers. Joe had a black eye, and I had a couple of bruises. God knows what the Mexicans looked like. There were no papers the next day because it was Christmas. I used the extra time to polish the story. All the time I was typing, my wife Avril complained about me looking like a prize fighter. Avril mellowed when she saw the story on the front page. If it had not been for the scoop, my story and this one great picture from Joe, I would still be scraping a living.

Captain Dudley Liam Smith was the reason I was at the police station that Christmas Eve. He talked the same to everyone, like they were equals. This included me, a reporter without prospects. Dudley Smith liked looking after people or at least some people. His men liked him and they were loyal. People conceded Smith was slippery, but he only pushed around the guilty they said, and in a modern police force you had to break eggs. The police were a line of defence, and to stand firm that line needed tall men with straight backs and wide shoulders. That was what they said about Captain Dudley Liam Smith but not after the boys in the press got the whisper he was responsible for the Nite Owl murders and shot Sergeant Jack Vincennes through the heart. Back then and before all that everyone rated Captain Dudley Liam Smith.

People ask me how long it took for the LA newsmen to realise they were being given a line about how Smith died a hero. About fifteen seconds, I would say. We were already wise to District Attorney Ellis Loew and the Police Chief and their lies. The Press went along with it because we thought the last thing Los Angeles needed was the whole truth about an underpaid and unqualified police force. And the Police Chief and DA made promises to our editors about rooting out corruption.

I was only in the police station that Christmas Eve because I had given Smith the benefit of the doubt at a crime scene months before. A deaf and dumb guy had been shot in the shoulder. He was sitting in an Oldsmobile and, unfortunately for him, there was fifty thousand dollars on the back seat. The deaf and dumb guy was running hot money across the city for Mickey Cohen. Captain Dudley Liam Smith compounded the money but let the guy go. Smith said the money would go to a good cause and the poor deaf and dumb guy needed a break. I looked the other way because there was no point in not. After Dudley Smith was killed that night in the shootout at the Victory Motel everyone looked the other way.

Whether I was right or wrong that time I watched Captain Dudley Liam Smith drop fifty thousand dollars on the front seat of a police car, it was my tight lips that got me into the police station that Christmas Eve in 1952. I have had a comfortable and interesting life and for that I have to thank Dudley. He always said the same to everyone, call me Dudley. Being so tall, he could afford to be friendly. Even when you called him Dudley you were paying respect. You felt it in the tilt of your neck. He had this soft Irish accent which meant you listened. His parents were definitely Irish but whether Dudley ever visited the place I do not know and I never asked anyone. Whatever you think or they say about him, Dudley was not small time.

Those days Mickey Cohen controlled LA and he had powerful friends out in Vegas. The cops wrapped Mickey up in a tax evasion charge and sent him to prison. The witnesses in LA may choke in court but the numbers cannot lie. Cohen had protection called Johnny Stompanato but Johnny was not much. He took up with Lana Turner and liked to keep her within reach which was unfortunate for Lana because Johnny was handy with his fists. Stompanato followed Turner to England where she was making a not so great movie with Sean Connery. James Bond movies were not then what they are now and Lana had wrinkles and pounds that John Garfield never saw in The Postman Always Rings Twice. Because he thought Connery had ideas about Turner, Johnny took out a gun and waved it in the face of the future super-spy. Connery knocked the gun to the floor and bent back the fingers of the right hand man of Mickey Cohen. We said in the War that the Brits were crazy. The point is Cohen was taking chances relying on Johnny Stompanato.

Pierce Moorhouse Pratchett owned a call girl service and invested money in schemes that were so high risk they were crooked. Captain Dudley Liam Smith and Pierce Moorhouse Pratchett rated Stompanato about as highly as Sean Connery did but it still took guts for Dudley and Pratchett to muscle into the territory of Mickey Cohen and move smack around the city. But they did. All these years later I wonder what would have happened if Ed Exley had been posted anywhere but LA and away from our own particular breed of angels. These days no one has a good word to say about Edmund Exley and even back then no one really liked him. Exley married a Mexican girl called Inez Soto. She had been raped and beaten by three black guys. I see this hard case cop Bud White once a year when he leaves his home in Bisbee, Arizona and returns to LA to drink and remember. Bud says Exley married Inez because he thought it would help his career.

There was much to admire about Ed Exley but he had his faults. They were different to those of Dudley but both men had too much ambition. Dudley wanted everything, money, a career, God knows what else, and on his good days he even enjoyed putting away the criminals. Apart from him and his friends of course. Whatever Captain Dudley Liam Smith saw he had to have, and, because he was a soft talking polite Irishman, no one saw him that way. Edmund Exley just wanted to be the greatest policeman there had even been on the planet Earth. We all knew why and maybe we should pity him. Edmund had to be the equal of his father. But no one can live up to the memory of a cop who was killed while protecting the best of the folk of LA. Edmund Exley never cleaned up the LA cops like he said he would but no one else did either and Ed did have his heroic moments. Edmund shot the three guys that raped the Mexican girl he later married, and Bud White, who could never hold his tongue after a few drinks, claimed that it was Ed Exley that killed Dudley Smith. Shot him in the back, according to White, but no one, including Bud, ever criticised Ed Exley for that.

Not one bad word passed between Dudley and me but all that was before we heard about the Nite Owl murders. Six people shot just to kill this cop called Stensland who with an ex-cop called Meeks had stolen a load of heroin from Dudley and Pierce Pratchett. Smith was behind all of it. Police corruption exists everywhere but what we had in the city of angels was special.

Whatever Bud White says, I reckon the real reason Exley married poor Inez Soto was because he never forgave himself for shooting those three black guys. Exley was suckered into thinking they had committed the Nite Owl murders. Later, though, Ed found out that corrupt cops on the orders of Dudley created the carnage in the Nite Owl. Then those cops took the shotguns they had used in the restaurant and planted them in the car of one of the three black guys. Ed Exley must have asked himself more than once whether he would have shot those guys if he had known that what they really did was rape and beat up a poor Mexican girl. If I'm right, Ed Exley needed to live and suffer with Inez Soto. That way he convinced himself he was justified in pulling the trigger and slaying those three guys even if he had been wrong about them. The marriage between Inez and Edmund was not a happy one. Inez wanted love, and Edmund Exley wanted a career. Odd to think that the Nite Owl killings ruined his marriage and probably saved mine.

Bud White says that Ed Exley was the cop that Dudley rated above them all. There were times when Dudley hated Ed for his straight necked ways but no one including Dudley Smith ever underestimated Ed. Dudley was always willing to praise Exley. The nickname Shotgun Ed came from Dudley. Another town and another Christmas Eve and it might have been different for Captain Dudley Liam Smith and Edmund Exley. This is what I sometimes think when Avril smiles at me.

DAVE ANDREWS

THE LAS VEGAS STORY
USA 1952
DIRECTOR – ROBERT STEPHENSON

Ain't no scope for embezzlement driving a taxi which is why I won't condemn Lloyd Rollins. Don't knock somebody for doing something if you ain't ever been tempted. Rollins was a gambler and handled big money for this firm back in the east. The guy had the opportunity. Me, I keep my own tips, and the rest is on the clock. Before the cab and before I came to Vegas I worked delivering newspapers around Los Angeles. I've always liked to move around. Ma was right on that one.

Get a job where you can move around because you won't ever be any good standing still, she said.

Ma figured me that way because I'm a talker. What Ma didn't say was I needed to move around and talk to people. I came to Vegas 'cause I thought LA was making me miserable, the concrete and the smog and everything. But it wasn't nothing to do with LA or me needing sunshine and desert. I just wasn't meeting enough people. I'm a talker.

Detective Lieutenant Sergeant Dave Andrews wouldn't say no to what I heard in the cabs but Dave was a guy that had to have the end before the beginning. Impatient is not the word for Detective Lieutenant Andrews. Now, Lloyd Rollins, he was different to Dave Andrews or at least he was to me. Lloyd Rollins listened to what I had to say and he was a generous man. Of course later we heard how none of it was his own money.

Sure I remember Linda Rollins returning to Vegas. Most of us talkers have good memories. I've thought about this. I reckon talking to people exercises what's up there inside your head.

That afternoon I had driven Howard Hughes to some airfield out there in the desert. Howard Hughes, you betcha, a special day all right. The guy made me wait around while he flew one of his airplanes. Imagine waiting all day with the meter running while this nutty guy is flying all over Nevada. It wasn't the most fun I ever had but the sight of the meter going round and clocking up the dollars and cents consoled me sure enough. I appreciated the cash Mr Hughes put in my hand but I didn't take to the man. The guy was full of himself but he did have Ava Gardner for company, and I reckon if she'd have been hanging on to me I might have got a little carried away. Not that she was hanging on to his arm. Whatever had happened between the two it was turning sour. There and back to the airfield Mr Hughes was talking the whole time about how he'd kicked off this commie writer from the picture he was producing. It sure as hell annoyed Miss Gardner. More than once she'd elbow him in the ribs and tell him to shut up about the damned commies.

Lloyd Rollins and Linda arrived that same evening. I was waiting at the train station, sitting in my cab and working out what I'd earned that day being a chauffeur for Mr Hughes and Miss Gardner. Mr Hughes may have been happy to spend money on waiting cab drivers but he wasn't much of a tipper. But I was happy. If you ask me, Mr Hughes wasn't much of a man. The next time I saw Miss Gardner in Vegas she was strolling around with Frank Sinatra, which I thought was a waste on account of how Sinatra wasn't tall enough to look into those gorgeous eyes. You see all sorts in Vegas, and not all the ladies cost as much to keep as Miss Gardner. He came to Vegas right until the end did Mr Hughes. He had some bungalow complex filled with his women, like a harem. There were just too many dames out there in that place for them to be all as expensive as Miss Gardner.

But I didn't need to be taken out to some airfield by one of the richest men in America and his movie star to remember Linda arriving. I liked Linda. I was saying the same to Dave Andrews down at the sheriff's office, how her face always promised a wink even when she wasn't smiling or anything. Dave told me I was out of line and he may have had a point because by then Dave and Linda were married. This, of course, was after the business with Lloyd Rollins.

Well before Linda hitched up with LLoyd Rollins she had walked out on Dave after he went to fight in Korea. And she went where most people go when they leave Vegas. She left the riverbeds for the angels. You get my meaning? Vegas means riverbeds in Spanish, and Los Angeles means, yeah okay. I talked to Mike, the guy that now runs the Last Chance saloon just off the strip. I said, why did he think Linda left Vegas as soon as Dave was posted outside the States. Mike pulled a long face like he does and said something about Linda not being able to settle in Vegas without Dave and the only way for her to move on was walk out on the both of them. It don't make much sense to me.

But after they locked up Lloyd Rollins for embezzlement and after Dave proved that Rollins for all his faults did not kill Mr Clayton there was enough good news for Linda to settle down in the desert city. Mr Clayton, and not Mike, was the guy that was running the Last Chance when Linda came back to Vegas. Clayton bought this necklace off Rollins who was in town and hoping to win some money to pay off what he had embezzled from his bosses up there in Boston. It don't make sense to me, rolling dice in Vegas when it was playing the odds that got Rollins into the mess in the first place. But I'm not a gambler. Some guys stuck outside an airfield in the Nevada desert would have passed the day reading about the horses. Not me because to me a gambler is a guy or maybe a dame that likes winning a dollar more than he hates losing one. Good, eh. I should write that down.

Where am I? I have to say, son, you sure are a good listener, nothing like Dave Andrews. That's right. Rollins sold to Clayton this necklace Rollins had bought for Linda back in LA. Clayton buys it for a fraction of what it was worth because Rollins had to have a stake for the crap tables. Clayton is thinking his ship has come in when he realises it ain't all fun having money because someone comes along and kills him and takes the necklace.

Everyone thinks the obvious. That high roller Rollins has killed Clayton and took back his necklace, thinking that maybe being given ten percent of what it was worth was not such a good deal. Meanwhile, Linda and Dave have got friendly again. I know because Linda rang Dave while I was at the Sheriff's office talking to Dave about what I knew about Rollins and the rest. I remember because he got angry with me mentioning my special day with Mr Hughes and Miss Gardner. But that was Dave, always impatient. And then Linda rings and the face on Dave changes into something that belonged to a kid on Christmas Day. He didn't talk to Linda like he talked to me, I can tell you.

Dave did himself no harm with just about everyone when he worked out who'd really killed Clayton and took the necklace, even if afterwards more than a few folks said that they'd known all along that Tom Hubler was up to no good. Hubler was this private eye from LA. Hubler had his problems because of what he put up his nose and down his throat which may be why he had to keep shooting people. All for the sake of a necklace, I ask you. Dave chased him out to the same airfield I had taken Mr Hughes and Miss Gardner but why Hubler drove all the way out there I couldn't tell you because Tom Hubler didn't have a plane to catch. There was a fight in the middle of the airfield, and it wasn't just Dave that said so because there were witnesses.

Dave whupped this Hubler guy which meant we had a happy ending, and happy endings ain't that common in Vegas, I can tell you. Mike got the Last Chance back because Clayton, the guy who swindled Mike out of the saloon in the first place, was lying dead in the mortuary and probably still wondering what the hell happened to the necklace. Rollins was still in prison, so he wasn't over the moon, but at least he'd made a detour around the gas chamber. Rollins was on a roll because he had this smart lawyer come up from LA to defend him in the embezzlement trial. Rollins was found guilty but this Fred Barrett guy had some psychiatrist talk about the horror of a gambling addiction. Barrett had the jury, the judge and all of them weeping. The foreman of the jury pleaded for leniency, and Rollins got off light, a couple of years inside the Nevada Penitentiary. Linda and Dave hooked up again and married. By the time of the wedding Dave was Sheriff and back in uniform. Dave left the badge at home but took the uniform to the wedding. Linda didn't wear white, just some two piece suit that didn't hide anything of what had got Dave interested in the first place.

A happy ending meant we were all happy, all except the piano player at the Last Chance. If he could tinkle the piano, it no way put a smile on his face which was why he was called Happy. The piano player thought the country was going to the dogs. The way he talked about the commies reminded me of that day at the airfield with Mr Hughes and Miss Gardner. Happy and Linda were always going on about the Red menace. They voted for Goldwater in '64. If it had been Dave, I'd have understood, seeing as he's been in Korea and he was Sheriff and all but Dave said he'd never vote for a President that was a warmonger.

So what's going on with Happy and Linda? I said.

Pay them no mind, said Dave.

Linda had a kid but she was nothing like her mother. Linda called her a pinko. Dave didn't like Linda talking that way about her own daughter. I know, I know. I'm going on. I said I was a talker.

FRED BARRETT

ANGEL FACE
USA 1952
DIRECTOR – OTTO PREMINGER

It's a pleasure to be called Shirley, thank you. So much of my life I've been called Miss Preston. Mr Barrett always called me Miss Preston. He was very formal, of course. His good manners might have had something to do with his first name. I know he hated being called Fred. His friends at the golf club would ring and ask to speak to Fred and sometimes they would call at the office and I would hear them say Fred to his face and slap his back. Mr Barrett would smile because he smiled at everybody but I could tell he hated being called Fred. I felt that Mr Barrett spent his life trying to be someone other than Fred. His dress was impeccable, and I don't think I ever saw a crease in his double breasted suit, a hair out of place or a day when his moustache was not trimmed just perfect.

Perhaps that was why Mr Barrett enjoyed being a lawyer so much and why he was so good at it. In court he was Mr Barrett, and there he could be what he wanted. Not that I ever had the chance to see him in the courtroom. My working life was restricted to the office. Mr Barrett called the office his backroom. I enjoyed the work. I typed complicated documents, met his customers and organised the diary for Mr Barrett. I even had my own assistant. Working for Mr Barrett was my second position after I left secretarial school. I stayed with Mr Barrett until I retired. I even followed him from Los Angeles to Las Vegas when we moved the office out there. That was a big decision for me but I thought why not. I would only be swapping one boring suburb for another.

I also knew Mr Barrett would look after me. He was a criminal lawyer but, because of his sharp brain, he understood corporate law. Mr Barrett always had one eye on the assets that belonged to his clients, and every time there had to be a clause in his fee that would provide an added bonus for the company. He arranged and managed my pension fund which is why I am so comfortable now. If he was always looking to grow the income of the business, Mr Barrett was not mean with his employees. He wanted everything in the firm to be top class. He paid good wages, and I had to fit out the office with the very best furniture available.

Although it was obvious Diane Tremayne had killed her parents, all the lawyers wanted to present her defence. The exceptions were those who worked in the DA's office. Young Diane was rich and beautiful and looked stunning in the newspapers. She was twenty three years old. The boyfriend was thirty five and he was, well, Frank Jessup was attractive. Frank was a tall and well-built man and he had been a racing car driver. A rich heiress falling for the chauffeur, you can imagine. The case was all over the Los Angeles Times. Of course, Mr Barrett was interested. Even if he had lost the case, the firm would have benefitted from the publicity. And there was not only the very high fee but the added bonus Mr Barrett could take from the funds left for Diane by her parents. Most lawyers would have simply taken the money and let Diane and her boyfriend go to the gas chamber but, no, Mr Barrett worked hard preparing a defence, although none of us expected a not guilty verdict. Well, Mr Barrett surprised us all and won.

I know people have said that it was my idea to have Diane and Frank marry inside the prison, marry so that the jury would hesitate about handing out a death sentence to two lovebirds. I wish the rumours were true but they are not. I do tell myself, though, that maybe I put the idea in Mr Barrett's head. For a while, when I was young, I used to read the society columns, and nothing interested me as much as the weddings of beautiful rich folk. One day Mr Barrett came out of his office and asked me to order him something for lunch. I was having my usual coffee and bagel and reading about this upcoming wedding between a movie star and a heiress. I oohed and aahed and said how exciting this wedding would be. Mr Barrett forgot his lunch order, and he asked me why so many people like to read about rich couples getting married. I told him that I could only speak for myself. I said seeing glamorous people in love and imagining them having lives that would not tarnish that love made me happy. Mr Barrett listened, nodded his head and stroked the side of his nose the way he did. Within the week Diane Tremayne and Frank Jessup were married inside the prison hospital.

It happened in the hospital because Diane had experienced some kind of nervous breakdown. Indeed it was a bedside wedding. Did the wedding convince a jury that Diane and Frank were an innocent couple? I doubt it but it must have swayed some of the members, those with hearts like mine. But the main problem for the prosecution was that their case relied on a car expert explaining how the car had been altered to cause it to reverse, crash over a cliff and kill Diane's parents. The truth is that the technical expert that can outwit Mr Barrett has not been born. And as Mr Barrett understood, few men like to think that another man knows more about cars.

I know Diane killed three people, four including herself, but I always felt sorry for the girl. I didn't like Frank's previous girlfriend, Mary, nor was I keen on Bill, the guy who was her alternative to Frank. Apart from Diane none of them were what I call loyal. Diane was such a small sweet thing, really beautiful. Then, that's me, I want rich people with big weddings to be happy. Today, Diane Tremayne would have been given psychiatric treatment. I suppose her love for Frank is best described as an obsession. Diane loved Frank Jessup enough to kill her step-mother. The poor father that Diane killed was in the wrong place at the wrong time. After the trial, and after they were released and when Frank went to the Tremayne home to collect his clothes and said no to her, Diane loved Frank enough to drive her and him over the same cliff where her step-mother and father were killed. If that isn't love, I don't know what it is, and every time I think about a desperate young girl putting the car into reverse and taking her and Frank Jessup to their deaths, well, it dries my throat. Some women, though, should learn to let go. My brother had a terrible time with his first wife. He didn't drive her over a cliff, of course, or alter the gear shift on the car of Mom and Pop. I would not say Frank loved Diane. He wanted her. Men can be like that.

I came to Las Vegas in 1964. I actually came ahead of Mr Barrett. That was an exciting time for me. I had to set up the new office and everything. Mr Barrett was sixty when we came to Vegas. The truth was that he was no longer so fashionable in Los Angeles. Mr Barrett said he had lost his edge. I was surprised he was not tempted to retire. He had enough money. I suppose I felt sorry for him, and that was another reason I came out to Las Vegas. Of course, he had identified potential customers well before we left Los Angeles. He had also decided that the firm would now take on bread and butter real estate work. We hired a young solicitor for that. Mr Barrett planned that whatever happened the real estate work would keep the company in the black. As it happened, Mr Barrett had plenty of criminal work. I thought he would be uncomfortable with some of our new customers but Mr Barrett had a smile for everybody even if it was only ever just a smile.

As he said to me one time, Miss Preston, I've had my back slapped by men who thought they were rough, now I have my back slapped by the genuine article.

There were no special deals in Las Vegas for the firm because none of our new clients had what you called corporate funds, and that was a disappointment. The new clients had plenty of money, of course, which was why they were willing to pay such high fees to the firm. I know that Mr Barrett became friends with Sam Rothstein. Sam managed the casinos in some of the hotels and he used to come into the office and show me his card tricks. I never

ever used formalities with our Las Vegas clients. Most of them preferred me to use their nicknames. Sam Rothstein was known as Ace, and even Mr Barrett was willing to call him Ace.

Towards the end there was talk of Mr Barrett standing for Mayor of Las Vegas. He had all the right connections. I can tell you, if he had stood, he would have been elected. But by then Mr Barrett was an old man.

This has come too late for me, Miss Preston, he said.

And he was right which, of course, was not unusual for Mr Barrett. He died when he was eighty-two years old. Mr Barrett was asleep and in his bed. Being Mayor of Las Vegas would have aged Mr Barrett, I think. Who knows, it might have killed him. I have just had a chill down my spine. I was thinking of one of the friends of Sam Rothstein. Nicholas Santoro was not a pleasant man, although all of our new clients were charming to me, even Mr Santoro. The stories about Nicholas Santoro that I heard, though, were terrible. Even just thinking about Mr Santoro and some of those stories, it sets my teeth on edge.

DAVE BANNION

THE BIG HEAT
USA 1953
DIRECTOR – FRITZ LANG

I'm a lucky son of a gun, believe me. Leaving the LAPD and joining the FBI was the best thing I ever did. I knew someone, and he told me about the kind of men they were looking for and what I had to say. You know the kind of thing. Back then in '53 the boys in the LAPD were a rough crowd. Dave Bannion was rough as well. Okay the guy knew how to put his body on the line and he could throw and take a punch. But Bannion was always different, which was why maybe nobody called him Dave. And Bannion had this idea he was the only straight copper on the force. This was not true. In Kenport District we had this guy called Cranston. and he was straight as the lines they were always telling us not to cross. The same guy, though, got by without throwing punches. Bannion was too ready with his fists.

If the LAPD had its faults, its training academy was always the best in the country. I was unusual. I listened to my trainers. One thing more than any stuck. I took it with me to the FBI and even quoted it to my recruitment board. The line between being a saviour and avenger is very, very thin, I was told, so it's best to forget about being a hero and just do the job the best you can.

Not sure if Bannion qualified as a saviour, look what happened to the women around him, but he certainly knew how to avenge. I once saw him reading this book by Mickey Spillane, something called I The Jury. Back then everybody read Spillane. God, back then people even used to read. Bannion didn't buy the book. I The Jury went around all the men in the District. The difference was that the rest of us read the book because everyone else was reading it. We all wanted to get to the ending that was supposed to be a stormer. Bannion was the last to have the book. That tells you something about how popular the guy was. I remember him reading it and drinking the coffee that yours truly had made him. He read this cheap paperback like it was the Bible or something.

Bannion was a Detective Sergeant, and didn't we know it. He had this big nameplate at the front of his desk and he thought being a detective and sergeant and all gave him the right for having someone make and bring his coffee. In his case the someone was me. He called me Hugo. You get it? You go for the coffee. I didn't like that. In the FBI I worked my way through the ranks but I always made my own coffee. Hugo, damn, no one was calling me by my right name.

No, no one was surprised that Bannion never made lieutenant. Those days the promotions were decided on the basis of the top three in these written exams that LAPD had for every promotion. Bannion was not the exam type. The guy didn't like any kind of examination from anyone. Bannion was given a lot of slack on account his wife was blown up inside their motor. People said all that changed Bannion but I saw no difference. The guy was always handy with his fists. Cleaning out the Laguna gang gave him respect but even without the exam system I reckon he'd have stayed a sergeant. Even in his finest moments Bannion was making mistakes. He said it was nothing to do with him but the guy had civilians protecting his daughter so that the hoods couldn't get their hands on her. Sorry but you don't involve civilians in police business. I don't care what's happening. Bannion even roughed up Tom Duncan's wife. True, the woman was crooked and in league with Laguna but she was still married to a cop.

And if Bannion did send Laguna to the can, he wouldn't have done it without Debbie Marsh.

Tom Duncan was a crooked cop and he thought like one. Mrs Duncan was cute and held on to the dirt her husband had collected on Laguna. She kept it inside her safe. The writing on the envelope said to be opened on her death. Guess what, Debbie Marsh plugs Mrs Duncan. Laguna would never have killed the Duncan woman because she had him nailed but Debbie, well, she didn't give a damn, not after her man had thrown a load of percolated coffee in her face.

Her boyfriend Vince Stone was a real stinker. He liked to put out cigarettes on women and when he really lost his temper he threw the coffee over Debbie. After that she ran to Bannion for help. He lent her the gun and hid her in a hotel but Debbie was on a mission. First, she takes the gun and blasts Mrs Duncan. Then she goes back home to Vince and this time she's the one throwing the coffee. Bannion arrived soon after but it was too late to stop Vince Stone firing two bullets in the belly of his girl Debbie. Bannion was given a medal for what happened next. He killed Stone in a shootout, and after the dirt in the safe of Mr and Mrs Duncan was found Laguna was tried and convicted.

Laguna said he was not a rough guy and he certainly didn't talk like a hood. His friends, and he had a few in LAPD, claimed he had a weakness. Laguna liked his henchmen to have wide shoulders and movie profiles. He was married and had a daughter but he had his other side. I don't have to spell it. Vince Stone wasn't as pretty as the rest, so I'm not sure what happened there, but he created more havoc than anyone. Having guys on your side that like to torture people is not a good idea. Laguna learnt the hard way.

People think Debbie reacted to living with this creep Stone, as anyone would, but I heard a tale. When she was younger, Debbie knocked around with Elizabeth Short, the dead babe they found in '47. Short was chopped in two, and her killer split her face from side to side. The Press loved it because it was gruesome. They called it the Black Dahlia murder. Vince Stone would have tested the patience of anyone but knowing what happened to Short affected Debbie, I reckon. After her pal was killed, Debbie liked to land the first punch, so to speak. And the girl was amenable to a drop of the hard stuff. That doesn't help. Neither did meeting Bannion help the poor kid even if he did mean well.

The women liked Bannion if the men didn't. But none of them ever lasted, and we all know what happened to his wife. She wasn't the first one to quit breathing. Some barroom girl was having this fling with Tom Duncan and told Bannion that there was no way that her dreamboat had committed suicide. Vince Stone heard the barroom girl had been talking. She was found dead in an alley after Stone had tortured her with cigarette burns. No one grieved over deadbeat Mrs Duncan but, of course, she kicked the bucket as well, thanks to little and soon dead Debbie. No, the women around Bannion didn't last long.

There was an exception, and this is what I want to talk about because, well, the Laguna business was a long time ago. This is what is odd. Guess what happens to Bannion. Well he goes no further than sergeant in LAPD, so what does he go and do? He only joins the FBI. He was always red, white and blue, and the FBI would have loved that. We didn't work together, thank God. He was based in the Las Vegas Unit. Bannion was impressed by what he saw in Vegas, the swanky hotels, the big acts and the freebies. I know all this because I met him this one time. He was older, and I remember he didn't have a grey hair in his head and he had all of it. We were both at some FBI conference in Kansas City. He kept talking about how great Vegas was and these days he wondered whether there was a price for progress whether you liked it or not. Bannion had a point. Since the mob moved out Vegas is not what it used to be. Say what you like about the hoods and them skimming from the casino rooms and everything but those guys understood customer service. They used to dish out freebies to the customers better than anyone. Providing you gambled you could get anything free, food, drink and for the high rollers even women.

Bannion didn't quite say the hoods were a mixed blessing but he'd changed. He just didn't sound like the Bannion I remembered. I knew he was different because he poured me a coffee.

Much later I mentioned my meeting with Bannion to someone from the old LAPD. He told me that Bannion had hooked up with some showgirl that was all curves and that before Bannion she knew people in the mob. Maybe that was the reason Bannion had to watch his step, said this guy. Maybe so but I definitely had the impression that Bannion had mellowed. People were different after the war. Not just Bannion wanted a better world then. When we got cash back in our pockets we all changed, maybe for the worse. The dame with the build had a bad car accident but the FBI people in Vegas believed it was rigged. The dame survived but the fabulous body and a lot more suffered. Bannion stayed with her until the end I heard. I don't have no details. I remember him, though. I don't dispute that. I wonder what ever happened to his daughter. She meant the world to him.

MIKE HAMMER

KISS ME DEADLY
USA 1955
DIRECTOR – ROBERT ALDRICH

Do I mind you smoking? You're kidding me. Of course I'll have a cigarette with you. Believe me, in my time I've had a lot more to worry about than Mike Hammer. Me, I would describe the man as direct. Mike didn't make concessions to no one. First, he wanted to know what was in it for him, and, second, he was rude to anyone that tried to mess him around. There are plenty of people who just don't get the idea or have their own messages. When that happened Mike could be handy with his fists, and I'd be lying if I said throwing his weight about didn't appeal to him. Mike and me were different but we liked one another. He was a good man to have on your side even if we clashed about what was the right thing to do.

Mike Hammer had this idea he could take the law into his own hands. I told him the police department couldn't and didn't tolerate that kind of thing and we wouldn't, even if he could scrape the dollars for a Batman cape. Mike hadn't even heard of Batman. He was offended by me mentioning comic books. More than once Velda claimed his taste was more sophisticated than his manner although I never saw Mike Hammer read a book. He liked good music, though. I remember that. He had this reel to reel tape recorder on the wall but that wasn't for music. He used it for telephone messages, the first time I'd ever seen anything like that.

Pat, he used to say, how the hell did you get to Lieutenant?

I said the same thing to him every time, I do my job and listen to what I'm told.

It made no difference. Mike always wondered if I might be sucking up to the guys that ran the department. Most of the time, though, Mike Hammer gave me the benefit of the doubt. And when he took the law into his own hands I bawled him out but I always covered for the bruiser or I did as much as I could. He took more knocks than he should have but that was because of the way he operated. Mike was no Sherlock Holmes. He liked to push people around and get his information that way. And he did it because he could which meant he often pushed around people that already had enough problems. Sometimes, though, he looked out for them. He had a soft spot for this Greek mechanic that fixed the cars, not that it did the Greek guy any good. Mike liked to drive fast convertibles but he had no idea what was under the hood. My boss said something about how Mike Hammer was too interested in machines that had power he did not understand. If only Mike had stayed away from fast cars and that cursed box that blew up all of Malibu Beach.

Mike Hammer may have been small-time but he won most of his battles. Of course like everyone else in his line he had to do his share of divorce work. The guys in the Crime Commission gave Mike a hard time over how he earned his living but a guy has to eat. And the same went for Velda. She led the husbands on because Mike asked her to and because the two timers were there to be led. Did she sleep with the guys to get the grounds the wives needed for divorce? I don't think Mike would have let Velda do that. He had a thing about the lady even if most of the time he kept her at a distance. Mike Hammer didn't like to mix business with pleasure although after he had been put into hospital for three days he did weaken and let Velda get close. Looking back, in view of what happened, I'm glad he did. Mike and Velda were entitled to a little comfort before they died. I wonder if Velda would have led the husbands so far if Mike had paid her more attention.

Of all the guys to get cancer I thought Mike would have been the last in the queue. Losing out to cancer was not in the script for two fisted Mike Hammer. Do I think it had something to do with the explosion on Malibu Beach? You're kidding me. First, both Mike and Velda died of high grade leukaemia, second, the whole of Malibu Beach and a lot more besides were turned to cinder. How the fire department even got Mike and Velda out of the ocean is beyond me. It must have been all hands to the pump or in this case pumps.

I know the rumours, how Mike Hammer and Velda are supposed to be up there in New York doing their best to clean up the city and avenge the victims they find. Let's try to talk sensibly. First, I like the stories as much as anyone. Second, Mike is as old as me and I've been retired for a decade. Even if he were alive he wouldn't be walking the streets and fighting criminals, more likely making coffee for Velda. Third, Mike and Velda went to New York for hospital treatment. That was the only reason. The doctors back east said the same as out here, high grade leukaemia. Fourth, not only has no one been allowed on Malibu Beach since it happened, the highway past Malibu is still blocked off. What was in that box may not have quite blown up the world but we are talking about serious radiation. There is more chance of JFK being alive than Mike Hammer.

Mike and me would have the odd beer together. I was a cop that went by the rules. Mike had his own code. A beer helped us forget our arguments. There was this jazz joint in Bunker Hill he liked, and, you know something, the folk in that place liked him. The club had this lady singer. She sang this tune that Mike rated, something about rather having the blues than what you've got. There was plenty of work in Los Angeles in the '50s and plenty of clubs and bars. People had money to spend but they had plenty to worry about as well. There were unwashed beatniks, and kids were going to hell. We had all this stuff with the Russians and nuclear bombs. On the TV we had to watch programmes about how to build bunkers for the nuclear fallout. And for those who didn't want to think about such things one of our neighbourhoods was called Bunker Hill except all the mansions up there were being used as flop houses.

California has plenty of beaches and plenty of sunshine but we had enough sad cases renting rooms out in Bunker Hill for cops like me to wonder about our supposed good times. I've worked in the LAPD all my life, and that's the difference between Mike and me but what we had in common was what we saw. And that was the crooks for whom good times would never be enough and the losers living lives as lonely as the dollars in their pockets. See that every day and you wonder if the old blues might just be better than what you've got.

I wonder if all that had something to do with why Mike couldn't let go of the business with Christina Bailey. In the beginning Mike thought there was money in it for him but when I told him that the government was involved he still continued poking his nose around which surprised me. The whole business was weird. Mike takes a phone call from a science fiction journalist that has disappeared, and I'm told to bring Mike into line because there is a missing box that is a serious leftover from the Manhattan Project. But women make a difference to everything. Picking up a woman wearing nothing but a trench coat is something you don't forget, especially when it happens in the middle of the highway late at night. Mike couldn't abide anyone that killed a woman, especially if the man got away with it. Hearing Christina Bailey tortured the way he did would have affected Mike. And he was frantic when Velda disappeared.

It's true. He did hand over to me the key to the locker where he found the box. Mike was like me. First, we are Americans, and second, we don't like commies. The Russians have a nuclear bomb, so there's no reason why we shouldn't have ten is the way I see it. Let's keep the world safe. Mike wouldn't have crossed the government and his country. The bad news for Mike was that the bad guys got to the box before we could. Who were the bad guys and how did they get hold of the box in the first place?

Plenty of important people have been curious. We'll never know. The head guy was rumoured to have been a doctor. A guy in a bar said something odd to me the other day. Imagine, he said, one of these days we'll blow up the planet in a nuclear war. No one will be left, and no one will know who is to blame because everyone will be dead. I've thought a lot about what he said. We couldn't point a finger at who caused what happened at Malibu, so a whole apocalypse would leave no trace. It doesn't seem right that afterwards no one will be able to say who caused the end of the world. I just hope that I'm not around.

SUPERMAN CLAUDE

MURDER BY CONTRACT
USA 1958
DIRECTOR – IRVING LERNER

I thought he was cute, cold but cute. In the kind of work I do, most of the men, well, I would not call them cute. Maybe they were once cute, when they were a bit younger perhaps but the time they get round to opening their wallet for me, well, they ain't so cute, so if a guy is cute and not so old, well, you don't mind so much him being a little cold except Claude was not a little. Claude was a lot cold. Now I know a lot more about Claude, well, that coldness I remember, it gives me the shivers, knowing he killed people for no reason other than he wanted money to buy his dream house, although why he wanted a big fancy home when he had no one to share the place doesn't make any kind of sense to me. Claude also kind of gave me the shivers that one time we met, when I had no idea what was to follow, but they were a different kind of shivers to the shivers I have now because I know now what Claude did to earn his money. I'm smiling because I know you know what I mean. And I smile a lot. I'm that kind of a girl.

You know, I can't even remember if Claude ever told me his name. I wouldn't have said he was a Claude. But after he was killed and they then traced the Mr Brink guy and it all came out, well, we all heard plenty about Claude. If Claude was as smart as Mr Brink said, it doesn't make much sense. Whatever, Claude was cute. Most of the story was in the papers but I know more than most, seeing as I have a friend in the DA's office. This gentleman I could not describe as cute and he is definitely not cold. No sir, but that's okay. I like a man that pays you attention. I enjoy being admired and, well, liked. Some men want you to stare at them all night or sit there like a dummy while they play the leader of the pack. I have a friend, she was taken to dinner by Mickey Cohen a few times. Well, the state of her the next day.

I said to her, I don't want no work with the likes of Mickey Cohen, thank you. No, sir, give me the quiet guy who is a little bit shy and wants to pay a girl attention, a guy that likes being with me, a guy that can look at me and be happy.

I'll be honest I've thought about Claude more than I have most men, which is odd considering we spent no more than ten minutes together. But Claude was different. I knew it the moment I saw him and I don't mean handsome although he was that and built like an athlete. But the whole time I was in his room Claude was, like, locked into something inside his head. Claude gave me a couple of drinks, big ones, and I took them because of how I could see he was in his own space and because I thought the booze might be able to help me reach out to him. The booze worked, and, well, I reached for him but I missed, which I could have predicted because Claude knew how to step out of the way. Some men do but they ain't the ones that invite you out to dinner. I wonder now why I'd been invited or even if it was Claude that did the inviting.

The whole time I was with him, Claude moved around, always finding somewhere else to stand by himself. A part of me didn't like it but, I have to be honest, a part did because, well, men, as a norm, do not step out of my way. The opposite if you know what I mean. And believe me most men do not cancel a dinner date with me, and not after meeting and seeing me. I asked to see him again, of course, and why not, I like to keep a full schedule and Claude was awfully cute and I hoped that without a train to catch next time he might be different.

I read all about what that Mr Brink said about Claude and how they called Claude 'Superman', but, of course, by then Mr Brink was facing the rap for hiring Claude in the first place, so Mr Brink would say things. When the trial of Mr Brink started I worried they'd call me as a witness. But my friend in the DA's office came good and they left me out. The next time I saw my friend I showed my appreciation. He left me that night ten years younger, dear me. I know what you mean, you wonder if their wives notice. Not that I wonder too much about their wives. I don't see why I should. They might want to look like I do but none would swap with me. So why should I feel sorry for them?

This woman that Claude was hired to kill was a piano player, so the papers said. She had a man's name, Billie Williams. I've wondered what that must be like. Not one of my friends has the name of a man but if one had, in this kind of work, she'd have to change. I would anyway. This Billie was asked what went through her mind when Claude appeared in her home and tried to kill her.

I was a little afraid, she said.

A little, can you believe it? I'd have been terrified. But this Billie said something, and I don't know why but it gave me those shivers I mentioned. This Billie said that she hoped Claude wouldn't kill her and that something inside her half believed that he might not.

His plan was to strangle me, she said, and I prayed he'd be just too shy for that, he'd pull back before he touched me.

The words she used were that he'd want to keep his distance. This Billie said that she had this idea that if she kept playing the piano it might just make Claude hesitate. And that made me think about how he'd been with me, how Claude had wanted to preserve his own space. What this Billie Williams said didn't make much sense to the men in court but they weren't women and they weren't going to understand how a woman can keep a man at a distance, especially if the man's heart isn't really into getting close.

This Billie Williams said something else that not everyone picked up on but my friend in the DA's office did because he told me about it. This Billie Williams said she found it impossible to imagine dying in the middle of a tune. Whether that included tunes she was just listening to, I do not know, but that is some imagination, which is what I said to my friend in the DA's office. But my friend said, and it just shows you, you think you know people but you don't because he said he couldn't imagine dying before he finished whatever book he happened to be reading. And I thought about this and I have to admit there is something I can't imagine dying in the middle of but it ain't reading a book or hitting the ivories.

Whatever was going on between Billie and Claude something made him hesitate long enough for the police to stop him. Claude ran and was killed trying to escape down the drainpipe. The cops pumped the pipe full of gas and bullets, and there was no more Claude which is kind of sad because no one wants to die in a drainpipe even if the fancy name for a drainpipe is culvert. If I'm going to die, let it be in the middle of a tune or some book even if it's not supposed to happen that way. But definitely not in the middle of a drainpipe nor halfway through the something I was thinking about before. Mr Brink was not for saying much in court but it came out that Claude had not been a contract killer for that long. This Billie Williams would have been the third person he killed. Claude would have had to kill a lot more before he could afford his house which may mean that there are now people walking around Los Angeles who could have been dead. But it is also kind of sad for Claude. The poor guy didn't even kill enough people to find the deposit on his dream house.

After what happened to Claude and in particular after I thought about what might have happened to me I never felt the same about Los Angeles which is one of the reasons why I'm heading to Las Vegas. I have a friend out there, Ginger McKenna, a beautiful girl who knows important people, except the only important people out there in Vegas ain't my kind because I'm the kind of girl that likes a man to pay attention and not always be being the great I am to his friends. But Ginger thinks she can fix me up with a job as a showgirl in one of the big shows. Why not, I think, I ain't the best dancer in the world but I can kick my legs in the air. I've had practice. I don't really like dancing that much. But if I'm honest, I'm a little worried about Ginger, and what are friends for if not to protect them from their latest steady.

And I do not like the look of this Sam Rothstein that has Ginger in tow. But that's another story. I need a change. After what happened with Claude, I'm not the same. I still like to be looked at and to be admired but I think maybe some space between whoever is doing the looking and me wouldn't go amiss.

MICHAEL CORLEONE

THE GODFATHER PART 2
USA 1974
DIRECTOR – FRANCIS FORD COPPOLA

Back then in '58 I was a young lawyer, corporate and finance, that kind of thing. I was nothing important but on a gravy train and glad to be earning good money. I wasn't making decisions, that came later and that was how I became a rich man. But back then in '58 I carried papers for the people doing the deals and I checked the contracts. My responsibilities were limited, and maybe that was a good thing because I did hear terrible things about the man. But the kind of people who ran Vegas back then, you can imagine. If I'd wanted nothing but fresh air, I wouldn't have decided to earn a living in Vegas. Not that I decided. My firm in Los Angeles sent me there. The job was something I had to do but it didn't bother me. By the time I was back working in LA again the main corporations had moved into the Desert City. If I was glad to return to LA, I have some fond memories of my time in Nevada. I liked the desert.

My acquaintance with Michael Corleone was limited to me being in the room on a few occasions and watching him do business, mainly with people who were legitimate contractors. Sometimes I would have to answer questions but most of the time I listened and watched my boss map the way forward. There was much to admire in Michael Corleone. Everyone including my boss warned me that Michael Corleone was treacherous but he was always straight in business meetings. And he was polite. I would say he was very polite. More than that, the word I'd use is cordial. He also knew how to flatter people. He would usually praise someone just before he asked them to do something.

It became predictable but why not, I thought.

Michael Corleone always made it clear what he wanted and he did not haggle. The man always paid top dollar. And he liked to put margins into the budgets. That is not unusual but Michael Corleone put in big margins, ridiculous really. He was that kind of man. The cost of a project did not faze him but he was horrified by the idea of not coming in under budget which, of course, was why he put in the big margins. My boss had a theory about why Michael Corleone overestimated costs the way he did.

He is the kind of man, said my boss, that can't bear disappointing himself. And rest assured, we won't disappoint him.

I don't think we ever did. Michael Corleone never complained about the fees or the work we did although he made sure that no one was signed into the percentages of the profits. Michael Corleone was tough with the grifters and the local politicians who thought they could hustle him for a payback but if you provided a service or a job, did something useful, he was a fair man. So it seemed to me. Most of the time Michael Corleone talked straight.

The law firm I was working for arranged the contracts on this hotel deal. Michael Corleone already owned a few hotels back in '58 but he had actually wanted a stake in Vegas from the end of the 40s. Back then Moe Green was in cahoots with Hyman Roth, and between them they owned a decent portion of Vegas. Moe Green said no way was a Corleone buying a Vegas hotel. We all know what happened to Moe Green. I came along later when Michael wanted to add the Hotel Tropigala to his haul. We trod carefully. Hyman Roth still had a stake in Vegas but he was busy thinking about his business in Havana and that helped us. My theory is that Michael Corleone would never have worked his way into Vegas without what was happening in Cuba.

Yes, I did do some work with the lawyer Tom Hagen. I probably spent more time with Tom than Michael. The two men had known each other as children, and I know that Michael rated Hagen but I didn't think the Corleone lawyer was anything special. Hagen had patience, and in our line of work that should not be underestimated. But I've known and worked with a lot of characters that were much sharper than Tom Hagen. You only had to watch the two to realise how loyal Tom was to Michael. Tom treated his boss as if he was royalty. Tom Hagen was as much a high class errand boy as he was a lawyer. In that respect I have to give credit to my own boss.

He once said to me, Behave with me in the way Tom Hagen does with Michael Corleone and I'll sack you on the spot.

I liked my boss for that although the same man didn't like being contradicted. I remember Michael Corleone being fastidious. Everything had to be so, you know, the way he lit a cigarette and drank his coffee. In the meetings Tom poured the coffee and made sure Michael had water. No, I remember, not so much water. Michael Corleone drank a lot of club soda. I felt like I was watching a performance and seeing a man dressed for the part. I only ever saw him in business suits. He was a man that controlled his appetites. I wondered if that was how he managed people, that he understood how they needed more than he did. Michael Corleone certainly made a lot of money catering to human appetites. And what he knew about people helped him survive.

But I felt he wasn't comfortable in Vegas. Sometimes we had meetings in his house by the lake at Tahoe. Michael Corleone had bought the house once owned by Whit Sterling. This Sterling guy was before my time but we all knew about how he was murdered by a woman who a couple of years before had shot him in the stomach and stolen forty thousand dollars of his money. It's hard to believe that someone like Sterling who was so good at making money could be so stupid when it came to this woman. But we all have our blind spots, and once you let people get too close they become impossible to understand. I know from my own family. That is what I remember from Michael Corleone. He let no one ever be close. Even his casual remarks were rehearsed. I wonder if that was why Michael acted all the time like he was royalty. It helped him keep people at a distance. The house Sterling had owned was a desirable property but it was a lot more desirable and expensive after Michael and his sophisticated New York wife added extra buildings. I met his wife on just one occasion, no more than a couple of minutes. Tom led us all on to the terrace to show us the view of the lake and the mountains. Kay was there having breakfast. Some women would have been irritated but she just smiled and apologised for not being able to chat. Kay never came into Vegas, and when I saw her I understood why.

The general opinion was that Michael Corleone could read anyone, and that was how he maintained his power and grew his empire. I heard that Michael had respect for Sam Rothstein and Johnny Rosselli but no one else. The truth is that Michael Corleone was cagey with everyone. His sister Connie spent more time in Vegas than Michael. She was well known around the casinos and the hotels, and the rumour was that she was never seen with the same man twice and that they were all younger than her. But a woman doesn't have to do much in Vegas to get a reputation. I also met Michael's brother, Fredo, but you couldn't have a conversation with Fredo. He wasn't the sharpest but, worse than that, every time a woman walked by him the gaze of Fredo would follow her and his brain would drift away. You spent half the conversation explaining what had just been said. Fredo Corleone disappeared, and of course there were stories. But I can't believe that a man would kill his own brother, even one as useless as Fredo although he wouldn't have been so useless if he'd been able to accept being what he was, which was, it has to be said, not very much.

I had just one face-to-face conversation with Michael Corleone. We were in an elevator. We were not alone. No one was talking, and Michael, to break the silence more than anything, asked me if I had a family.

No, I said.

You have a wife, though? said Michael.

No,' I said.

I thought you were ambitious, said Michael.

I am,' I said.

The doors of the elevator opened and Michael stepped out.

He turned his head, looked at me and said, An ambitious man needs a family.

And that was it. The next day the boss assigned me to the Ace Rothstein contract. Ace, his real name was Sam, was a very different kind of man to Michael Corleone. He was in deep with this no good woman called Ginger but Ace couldn't let go. Not long after the few times I met Michael Corleone I heard he was divorced from his wife Kay, the elegant woman I had seen eating breakfast that one time. Michael wasn't like Sam or Whit Sterling with women. The ladies weren't given second chances. But then Michael Corleone was that way with everyone. I don't think about him that often but I've thought about Kay sitting on the terrace by Lake Tahoe and her eating a slice of toast the way she did that morning. How a lady with her style ever got involved with someone like Michael Corleone, I'll never know.

HANK QUINLAN

TOUCH OF EVIL
USA 1958
DIRECTOR – ORSON WELLES

Damned right I blame Hank Quinlan for what happened down there in Los Robles but not as much as I once did. Miguel had wanted me, back in the States, to get help from a psychiatrist or a counsellor or someone. I said no thanks and that I'd beat the blues on my own, thank you. But what happened down in Los Robles back in '56 still gives me nightmares. I just don't hate Hank Quinlan like I used to and I've learned to live with the nightmares. I hate them all for what happened. And when I say all I include me. God it was awful. The night Miguel and me arrived in Los Robles I was accosted by this Mexican hood. He was a handsome guy, and I called him Pancho which I shouldn't have, and he didn't like. But if I had my time to go over again, I would have called the punk something a lot worse. And then I was dragged to see this tough guy clown called Joe Grandi. I called him a stupid little pig which I definitely don't regret even though he was murdered later.

When I saw him the next night he was without the wig on his head and lying dead at the bottom of my bed in this fleapit hotel in the centre of Los Robles. I didn't feel anything but terrified. I woke up in the dark and I was drowsy from all the sodium pentothal that Pancho and his charming friends had popped into me that afternoon. I had been staying at the Mirador Motel which is out of town and in the desert somewhere. But as soon as I was knocked out by the sodium pentothal they dragged me into the fleapit downtown where Grandi was killed by Quinlan. I just wanted to get out of that fleapit fast. Quinlan and Grandi had this plan to make me look like a dope head. They had different reasons but the one thing they agreed on was that Miguel had to be discredited. And they went for what they thought was the weakest link, that is me. After what happened down in Los Robles, I now travel north on my vacations. It affected me which is why I talk too much when I meet people. Thank you, you're very sweet. You can't believe how proud I am of stopping smoking. I did it all on my own. By then there was no Miguel Vargas in my life. That's another story. I haven't smoked for some time.

I had expected peace and quiet in the Mirador. And I hate myself for that. I had insisted that Miguel take me to a motel back on the American side of the border. Miguel was annoyed, seeing as he was Mexican and working for the Mexican Government. If only I'd have stayed in Los Robles. At least I would have been close to Miguel, not out on my own somewhere. Funny thing, Los Robles had a strip joint. For a small town the place had some pretty girls. Overdone ladies perhaps but pretty, nevertheless. Miguel told me about this Norwegian guy that hung around the joints. His aim was to persuade some of the girls to follow him back to LA. You can imagine the kind of work he was offering. Miguel didn't mention a name. All he said was that this man had a big Adam's Apple.

Where was I? How could I forget? Grandi sent Pancho and his gang out to the Mirador and they assaulted and doped me. I can't describe how awful it was and if I could, I wouldn't. Once Pancho and his friends had me unconscious they dragged me back to Los Robles and dumped me in that terrible hotel. Miguel was busy on this case he should have never been involved in. Some local bigwig had been blown up in his car. He had a young woman with him, and she was pretty too.

To be fair to the Mirador Motel at least the bed had clean sheets unlike the fleapit where Grandi was killed. But then Norman Bates kept his motel clean, and look what happened there. The man that ran the Mirador was creepy but he meant no harm. What could he do against Pancho and his reprobates? There were a couple of girls in the gang but they were as twisted as the guys.

Can you believe that? Things have been said about the man who was in charge at the Mirador. He wasn't the type to take home to Ma and Pa but he didn't act hysterical in the way people said. People don't have to be gangsters to be cruel. He was creepy though. He had a look of the actor that played Norman Bates in Psycho. I went to see the film but I couldn't bear to watch it all the way through. A film about dark deeds in a motel brought back too many memories.

I was still with Miguel then. Miguel didn't make a fuss when I panicked in the cinema. Miguel was like that, he liked to be protective. He was a big man and a decent man which was why I married him. I felt protected which was maybe why I felt so let down by him. It wasn't really his fault but if he hadn't got involved doing the decent thing in Los Robles then none of it would have happened. The truth is that his decency wore me down in the end. He was always fighting a cause somewhere. See what I mean about blaming everyone and not just Hank Quinlan? People don't realise that I never met Hank Quinlan. Maybe if I had, he alone would be my monster. I heard all about him from Miguel and how Quinlan used to frame suspects. But I also heard about how his wife had been strangled to death and that Quinlan was never the same after that. He was some kind of man, I suppose.

Once Miguel discovered the police corruption in Los Robles then Quinlan had to do something or felt he did. And Joe Grandi wanted to discredit Miguel before the trial of this other Grandi that was in prison. That was why Quinlan and Grandi hatched the plan for Pancho and his friends to fill me up with dope. Miguel was a little vague when I asked him why did Quinlan kill Grandi. Miguel could be like that, preoccupied. Miguel said something about Hank Quinlan not wanting witnesses and Quinlan being off his head on booze and not being able to think straight. Quinlan killed Joe Grandi in the fleapit while I was there out cold in the same room. And with one of my stockings, would you believe. Honestly, that isn't the kind of thing that makes you feel good about yourself.

Los Robles was a dump of a town. The kind of scruffy place that looked less dangerous at night because you couldn't see the dirt and rubbish quite so well. But Miguel and me got a kick out of walking through the border crossing that first night. It felt like being free. That only lasted until the car exploded, and that was when Miguel got involved. I blame him for that. I blame myself for wanting to go to an American motel. I blame the other cops that let Quinlan run his crooked show even if they were hoodwinked. I blame any of the trash associated with Grandi. I blame the guy that ran the Mirador for not having the sense to jump into his truck and drive to get help. I blame the local politicians who had not wanted to ask questions about a local police detective who never failed to solve a case and had the good luck of always finding incriminating evidence. And I blame the girls in Los Robles who for a few bucks let these deadbeat men think they were something. All that doesn't let Quinlan off the hook but I can't just hate the one man. Maybe if I could it would have been different between Miguel and me.

Miguel quit his job in Mexico City after what happened in Los Robles because I wanted to come home to the States. I have nothing against Mexicans. Here in Los Angeles I work to support the Mexican communities and I've found good friends there. But after Los Robles I just needed something more familiar. Miguel agreed because he couldn't resist the idea of rescuing me again. I know I'm being harsh but it was how I felt about him and everything after what happened in the Mirador in the desert and then the fleapit downtown. You know, I like vacations but I've never stayed in a hotel since what happened in Los Robles. I made Miguel buy a big camper. Those were good holidays but they didn't keep us together. Now I rent a lodge in the Rockies every summer. Me and a couple of girlfriends. It's not quite the Rockies. It's not far from this town called Bridgeport.

Mike's job here in Los Angeles didn't help any, and after a while I think he blamed me. The feeling was mutual you could say.

Miguel worked for the District Attorney. I told him it was a good job but Miguel felt it was a comedown after working for the Mexican government. And of course he saw things he didn't like. I lost count of the times he said so much for American progress. Miguel used to say that Quinlan would have been thrown out of the LAPD for decency. There were cops in LAPD helping to run drugs over Los Angeles. The only cop Miguel had any respect for in LA was this detective called Dave Bannion but Bannion left to work for the FBI and after that Miguel couldn't settle. So I blame the damned LAPD for Miguel wanting to go back to Mexico and for the two of us separating. I did pack my case to follow Miguel to his job in Mexico but by the time the taxi had arrived to take me to the airport I had unpacked the case. A month later I was no longer Mrs Vargas. These days I keep away from men. I have a tennis instructor I like and I let him mix me a martini but I even keep my distance from him. He doesn't seem to mind. No, he's Mexican.

ACE ROTHSTEIN

CASINO
USA 1995
DIRECTOR – MARTIN SCORCESE

I remember you. We met in Los Angeles a couple of years back. Still working and writing, I see. We all have to make a living, I suppose. I told you all about that strange guy. That's right, Superman Claude, the guy they shot and gassed in the drainpipe. I still go back to LA a couple of times a year. I make my living here in Vegas. I don't kick my legs in the air anymore but I get by, and dealing cards on a blackjack table is a lot easier on the pins. Ginger McKenna, since departed, got me the job. That ain't strictly true. She spoke to Ace Rothstein, and he gave me the job. Ace had this idea of having female blackjack dealers to drive up the betting in the casinos which it did. I was one of the first women blackjack dealers in Vegas. Ace would have preferred someone younger than me but he knew I didn't look so bad. And the lights in the casino don't do the wrinkles any harm.

I know what people say, that Ginger McKenna should never have got married and that she was a working girl who should have stayed that way. I wouldn't say that was wrong but what I would say is that if she was going to get married it sure as hell shouldn't have been to Ace Rothstein. They were different people. Ginger was a beautiful girl, and Ace was, how do I put this, he looked like what some girls would think was a customer. You understand me? I can see from your smile that you do. Not that Ginger went for the oil paintings. Her first husband Lester Diamond wouldn't win a beauty contest either.

You shouldn't ask me about Ace and Lester. Ace was my boss. I've never been a fan of bosses, and in the casino everything had to be the way Ace said, you know, my way. The man wasn't always easy but he had respect. The FBI called me in to speak to them this one time. A guy called Dave Bannion. He had terrible things to say about Nicky Santoro which is understandable as Nicky was doing heists across the city and killing people. But Dave Bannion talked differently about Ace Rothstein, to the extent I wondered whether Ace had done a deal with the FBI. There have been rumours. But no one no way had respect for Lester Diamond. Ginger felt something for him, that's true, but I wouldn't call it respect. Lester was this skinny nervous guy and he set my teeth on edge but Ginger thought the clown had something. I saw Lester the first night I arrived in Vegas after Ginger had invited me out here. I didn't like Lester Diamond then and, as far as I could see, the creep got worse.

Ace and Lester both lived off people but in different ways. Ace was a fixer that liked to chisel the odds. You always got something from Ace but he took more than he gave because he was an operator. Lester just fed from people. And Ginger having Ace as a rich husband meant that for Lester there was a lot to feed from. Lester got more nervous and restless thinking of the money Ace had, and Ginger just had to feed the leech that hung from her arm. If I blame anyone for what happened between Ace and Ginger, it was the creep Lester. He never did an honest day's work in his life. Ace and Ginger were never going to make Ideal Homes as the married couple of the year but without Lester and his claws they might have stood a chance. And then maybe not.

I know this man. I won't call him a guy because he's a gentleman. He's a lawyer. I've known more than one lawyer in my time. This man talks to me sometimes. He doesn't play the tables and all the time I've known him he's never asked me for anything. He just likes to talk and buy me martinis. Mister Barrett was a big shot in LA and he's even done well here in Vegas. Without him that animal Nicky Santoro would have been sent to the pen for at least one of his fourteen murders. I haven't seen Mister

Barrett recently but I remember everything he said to me. We had this conversation about Ace and Ginger and the battles they were having.

People are talking about bad publicity for Vegas, I said.

It won't make much difference, said Fred Barrett.

I never called him Fred to his face, always Mister Barrett.

The people who run Vegas have been good customers of mine, said Fred Barrett, but they won't last out here in the desert.

At the time I knew Howard Hughes had bought his first hotel.

He will buy others, said Fred Barrett.

Hughes and Fred Barrett were working on half a dozen acquisitions.

Once that happens, said Mister Barrett, Wall Street will become interested.

I just listened.

The hoods won't help themselves, said Fred Barrett, and there'll be killings but there are always more hoods to replace the dead bodies.

Oh dear, I said.

That won't be the reason they disappear, said Mister Barrett. No, Howard Hughes won't own all of Vegas because he will become bored before that happens. But he is a lot bigger than a crack in the door, and once it's open.

Of course, I said.

Now, if I'd been married like Ginger, I wouldn't have heard any of that. Not that it would have made any difference to Ginger.

People play around everywhere, look astray, whatever words you want to use. But there is only one way to play around in Vegas and that is in public. Maybe it's because the place is surrounded by desert or maybe it's something to do with how the place is built to worship money. You need faith to survive in Vegas. And that faith means having money, spending it and having fun. Ginger and Ace both strayed. What annoyed them, though, was everyone else seeing them play around. There were arguments and fights but that could have settled into a routine except there was also Lester hanging on. As long as there was Lester, there was no equality between Ace and Ginger, no tit for tat. People ask me why she just didn't dump Lester. You know, Ace walks around thinking he knows everything but he didn't know that Ginger had a kid with Lester before she met Ace. Lester was the father of her first child. I think that was the reason she couldn't abandon Lester. And Ginger could also be herself with Lester. That makes a difference, too.

I talked to Mister Barrett about Ace and Ginger and asked him what I could do as a friend. Mister Barrett just looked at me and shook his head.

The problem with those two, said Fred Barrett, is that the husband earns his living by knowing you can't beat the odds and the wife can only get through life by trying to beat the odds.

I have to say, I've thought often about what Mister Barrett said. To me that sums it up well. Ace and Ginger were both hustlers but opposites. Ace calculated the odds and when he couldn't get them to work in his favour he cheated. That was how he became friendly with the mob. If he hadn't fixed so many fights, football games and horse races, he might have been given a gaming licence in Vegas which is what I think he wanted more than anything. Ginger didn't want the odds in her favour. She wanted to beat them. If she hadn't, she might have stayed off the coke and the booze. But she didn't, and that was what she had in common with that lowlife Lester Diamond.

You're going to ask me why didn't she leave Ace. She wanted the money. And, because she was my friend and did me favours, I like to think she had to be kind of loyal to any man that fathered her children. I know what you're going to say, the time she tied her kid to the bed so she could hit the town is no way for a mother to behave. I didn't say Ginger was a good mother. That doesn't mean, though, you can't be loyal. It works the other way, too. I've never felt loyal to a man in my life but I've always been fair, always been straight with them.

What did Ginger McKenna see in Nicky Santoro? Well, it wasn't his handsome profile, that's for sure. She did it with Nicky to get even with Ace. Nicky was a shoulder for a while and he was dangerous. Ginger always liked to beat the odds. And, when Ginger walked off with two million dollars that belonged to Ace, she must have thought she'd beaten the odds big style. And she did except she didn't. Lester, Ginger and maybe others spent the two million in a couple of months. Some of the same friends said it was an accidental drug overdose except, as Mister Barrett said, it was always going to happen. And I say that as a real friend. The way she lived, the way she wanted to live, it was always how it would end. Call it fate, the odds, whatever you want. Ace was right after all. You don't try to beat the odds. Ginger died when she was forty six years old. Ace lasted until he was almost eighty.

As Ace once said to me, whatever way you play you lose but there are ways of losing more slowly.

My shift is about to start. Nice to meet you again.

JOHNNY COOL

JOHNNY COOL
USA 1963
DIRECTOR – WILLIAM ASHER

The man backed himself, big style. Give the guy credit for that. But that was his problem, man. Johnny Cool was a dice player, apart from when he was killing people, of course, and I never saw a crap player that lasted long. You want to know the first lesson I learned behind a poker hand? You can only back yourself for so long, man. You don't get far in this life if you don't listen to the cards. Johnny Cool was tough and smart. He bumped off four protected guys in one day, right here in Vegas. Johnny Cool blows up this guy in the middle of his own swimming pool. And the kids are watching. That is a heavy deal, that is what I call raising the ante. That is not listening to the cards. Johnny Cool was using exploding suitcases like depth charges. The guy was tough and smart, so tough and smart he thought he could play an inside straight. And what does Mr Hoyle say about inside straights. That's right, man, it's a no no. Always and always play the odds and listen to the cards. The bluff comes when you know the stars are in line. It happens because it has to sometime but you don't chase it. You keep your eyes open, man. Walk around the tables here in the Sands and what you see, what excites the tourists, are the high rollers. The guys with a wad who wouldn't know the difference between an inside straight and a three of a kind but for a night have struck lucky. But that's what people want to see. A guy on a roll who isn't listening to anything other than himself.

I said goodbye to the dice a long time ago. I quit the same night that Johnny Cool backed me with twelve thousand dollars. I'm not an excitable man. You can't be in this business without knowing how to feel the ice but I sweated that night, man, especially when Johnny Cool put a gun at the side of my head and said roll again. The weirdest thing was he was being friendly. Johnny Cool was showing how he believed in me. These days I'm strictly a poker man and I raise my own stakes. It's not so easy keeping your head down when you're a not so tall one eyed Jewish black brother but I don't need to stroll like some. I play Texas Hold 'Em because that's the only damned poker game in Vegas. The worst thing that ever happened to poker was Texas Hold 'Em but, what do you say, you have to go with the flow. I am a quiet one down and four up man but I can play any kind of stud poker. You just have to know when to hold and when to fold. And that was one lesson poor Johnny Cool never did understand.

Where did he get his handle from? Follow this, man, watch the dealer. There were two Johnny Cools. The original was a seriously loaded Italian hood from Chicago called Johnny Colini but nicknamed Johnny Cool. The FBI kicked him out of the country. They reckoned the lack of his presence on American soil might do something about organised crime. Some hope, man. Another crew moved in on his action or mostly the same crew but with a different head honcho called Vince Santangelo. The original Johnny Colini needed someone to get even with the guys back in the States. A guy with sense would have left the table and spent the rest of his days enjoying the good life and sunshine in Italy. But that's high rollers for you. They have to back themselves until the very end. The problem was that the guys back home held all the aces. So Chicago Johnny Cool, now in Italy, slides his own ace below the deck. He finds this Sicilian bandit that lives in the mountains and is so tough the police can only stand by and admire and whistle. This bandit is called Salvatore Giordano, and all the village folk love him because he fought the fascists and spits in the eye of just about everyone that wears a uniform. The story is that Salvatore killed a soldier that attempted to rape his mother. After that and a few dead fascists, Salvatore became a man of the people. Well, the only person that Johnny Cool, the original, looked after was called Johnny Colini. Colini picked Salvatore for one reason only. He picked the toughest guy in the neighbourhood.

The second Johnny Cool goes along with the first Johnny Cool because, if he didn't, the first Johnny Cool would hand the second Johnny Cool over to the Italian cops. Before Colini arrived with his helicopter to lift Salvatore out of the Sicilian mountains the cards had been kind to Salvatore Giordano. The man was carrying a really heavy wad. The last thing that Giordano needed was someone to come along and fold his hand but life is like that. Any poker player can tell you, man. There is nothing worse than having a good hand, a full house, four of a kind, a running flush or something and someone comes along and folds the hand before you make the final bet and pick up the pot. It's happened to us all. I once was dealt a running flush just before an earthquake arrived. And you know what sticks in my throat? It's people telling me I was lucky to get out of the place alive.

Forget the earthquake, let it rumble.

Back in Italy the first Johnny Cool teaches the second the American language, puts him in smart suits and gives number two the low down on what is happening back in the States. Johnny Cool two now knows the people that need to be taken out the game and what the game is that all these people are playing. This is why the new Johnny Cool arrives in Vegas. He stayed right here in the Sands. I spotted him right away but no one else took much notice of the guy. He played a few crap games and carried a wad of cash but so what. The real action starts when he goes to New York. Johnny Cool number two killed important people. He had inside information from Johnny Cool one and, man, he must have thought he was dealing from the bottom of the deck and had to win. The problem was he was in a game where everyone had information. They were all dealing from the bottom of the deck. It's not easy, man, you don't have an edge. You're just backing yourself, and even the cards are confused.

After the mayhem in the Big Apple our Johnny Cool two comes to Vegas and creates more of the same. Imagine, blowing up Lennart Crandall in the middle of his own swimming pool. Crandall was a handy swimmer. He practised every day. The poor guy may have been in bits when he died but at least he came to the surface. The tale is that Johnny Cool two considered Crandall to be mission accomplished and was on his way back to sunny Italy, job done. Maybe Johnny Cool two was bored with killing Americans and, as it happened, he had met one he rather liked, a good looking dame called Darien Guinness. No, she was loaded but not that rich, no connection with the booze people. Johnny Cool one wanted number two to take over the USA business on behalf of number one but according to this dame with the name like the black beer, Johnny Cool two and her were supposed to be heading to the Sicilian Hills to enjoy the quiet life.

Now I've got nothing against dames, and there are a few that have liked me. But I don't kid myself. Any dame is an inside straight, cards that always promise more than they can deliver. But just like an inside straight looks great when it is in your hand, it's the same with a dame. If you win, there is nothing better but you have to think of the odds.

Two of Vince Santangelo's men had roughed up the dame, well more than just being rough, and Johnny Cool number two had made sure they paid big style. There are no suspended sentences in the Sicilian mountains, man, you know what I mean. Something about Johnny Cool attracted this Darien Guinness. She said he was the only man that had never told her lies and she knew he was honest because what he told her was so terrible. But when she read about how the two kids had seen their old man Lennart Crandall dive out of the water instead of in, well, the dame knew although it had been fun with Johnny Cool the time had come to fold the cards.

Johnny and Darien were supposed to meet in some Italian restaurant in New York but Darien needed to call it quits and the best way she knew was to tell the hoods where to find Johnny.

They were waiting for Johnny Cool. Darien Guiness confessed to the cops that she had driven the car that Johnny used before he scattered Crandall over the pool. The babe looked sweet in court, and the judge gave Darien a suspended sentence providing she went for psychiatric treatment. The defence lawyer claimed the woman was a victim, and maybe she was because these days she works with children and raises money to support those places where drunks dry out. The rest you must have heard. Johnny Cool number one died in bed, not asleep I heard, something to do with a girl half his age. Johnny Cool number two had a hard time with the number of hoods waiting for him but he waited for the right cards to fall, one of those hands when the stars aligned, and somehow he got out of there. Johnny Cool number one, who at that point was still breathing, managed to get his boy out of the States. Johnny Cool number two doesn't get around much these days I heard but he is out there, somewhere in the Sicily mountains and with the people he cares about. No more inside straights for Salvatore Giordano, thank God.

LUCKY JACKSON

VIVA LAS VEGAS
USA 1964
DIRECTOR – GEORGE SIDNEY

THE KILLERS
USA 1964
DIRECTOR – DON SIEGEL

To be honest it wasn't so good before the crash but after Lucky came off the track and turned the car right over, well, it all went boom. No one was surprised by Lucky and Rusty having arguments after they married. Each was used to being the star of the show. Egos, they call it. The way Lucky had of giving orders didn't bother me none. I was the mechanic, and Lucky was the driver and the guy everyone wanted to meet. So, so what. Lucky Jackson had no fancy airs. And Lucky did know one wrench from another. I never met anyone who got a pair of overalls as dirty as Lucky Jackson could. The wrenches weren't the problem. The wenches, it was different. Lucky didn't play around, not after Rusty appeared, but Lucky and Rusty were handsome people and they got the smiles. Rusty was as cold as ice, and that helped the marriage but Lucky had a different nature. If a woman smiled at Lucky, he had to smile back. That was okay when everything was fine between Lucky and Rusty, a smile is just a smile, but when there were arguments Rusty remembered the friendly grins. Boom, it just made things worse.

Lucky and me worked on the cars together. We were as close as brothers. We had some good times but then Rusty came along and it was different. We won that race in Vegas okay but the next couple of times out Lucky had bad breaks and finished nowhere. Whatever Lucky and Rusty were arguing about at home it had an effect. Lucky lost his edge. He'd walk in the garage and he was a different man. I could tell. Before Rusty happened it was Lucky that was pushing me to work hard. After he got married it was me pushing Lucky. The racing trophies didn't line the shelves, that I remember. And, like Rusty, there is a lot of pride inside Lucky Jackson. Troubled or not, Lucky wanted to be the winner. Lucky took chances on the track because he was slipping and because he had to. It helped for a while. He picked up a couple of wins but the inevitable happened.

It wasn't all Lucky's fault. The other driver was in Lucky's space. But Lucky reacted and he was that busy worrying about this driver he messed up the bend. The car went straight up in the air. Lucky wasn't dead but the accident wrecked his left eye and the cost of the car repairs ruined me.

I told him in the hospital, Lucky, I'm broke and finished with all this, and you ain't going to pass no medical, so you can forget about driving.

We argued about it. We could have got jobs as mechanics working for this Italian count or something. Lucky said that me suggesting working for the count was not showing respect. I never saw Lucky Jackson again.

The rest I heard when I went back to Vegas for the big car race they have every year, the one that Lucky won in '64. I went to watch. No, I never married. I was there alone. The race Lucky won in Vegas, those were the best days, all of us pulling together. Who would have guessed that on the same exact day a year later Pops would die. That changed Rusty because when Pops was around he would tell his daughter to ease off worrying about car crashes. And she did. But after her father died, Rusty brooded about death and what could happen on a racetrack. The crash was not the final straw but it made the arguments worse than ever. Yet when Rusty had visited Lucky in hospital they acted like two people who remembered they loved one another. If they hadn't, I might have hung around. But I thought the guy doesn't need me.

It really blew up between them after he took the medical to go back into driving. Lucky failed like I said he would. So he starts driving under an assumed name even though Rusty had found him a spot in the Flamingo, the hotel Bugsy Siegel had built. She thought it crazy that Lucky was racing and was not best pleased she had to tell the folks in the Flamingo no deal. Rusty and Lucky had a row and said things. Lucky walked out on Rusty and said goodbye to Vegas. Not long after he was caught driving under the fake name, and after that he couldn't even get a job working in the pits. Boom boom. Lucky drifts around the small towns and gets by driving in junk heap races at county fairs where they ain't so particular.

Rusty hung on in Vegas and found new friends. Not good friends, that I know. One was Ginger McKenna, a gorgeous moll that wise guy Ace Rothstein had in tow. Having loaded friends kept Rusty working. She always had the pool job but funds came from the showroom spots, the kind of entertainment work that Rusty had wanted for her husband even though Lucky Jackson was no professional entertainer. Autos were his love. He didn't mind having fun on stage but applying himself to music like he did to cars, that wasn't Lucky Jackson. Rusty didn't forget Lucky which was why she got into bad habits maybe. Not the drink or the drugs like her friend Ginger. No, Rusty couldn't stop spending money. If a beautiful girl likes nice things then maybe Vegas ain't the place to be. The more money Rusty had the more she wanted. Did the men use her or did she use the men? Difficult question, mister. The men paid big style but then so did Rusty.

I don't know who came up with the idea. Rusty wanted money for the sake of it, and Ginger wanted money that husband Ace Rothstein wouldn't know about. Money for the coke and bourbon, I suppose. The plan was to rob a US Mail truck that took money from all the hotels on the Californian coast before dropping it in a bank in Los Angeles. The people Rusty knew, they needed a driver. Rusty with the help of Ace finds Lucky dragging a junk heap at some dump of a racetrack and makes the offer.

Lucky and this guy, it wasn't Ace Rothstein, this guy was called Santoro and bad news, Lucky and this Santoro guy would pose as cops and divert the US Mail truck off the main drag and on to a country road. In the pretend cop car they'd use to divert the Mail truck, Lucky and Nicky Santoro would then follow the truck, overtake it and, with the help of two guys waiting at the other end of the country road, rob the money in the back of the truck. The country road was not that long so the driver of the cop car had to be fast. But Lucky could do that kind of thing in his sleep and maybe he did.

They rob the money, and no one gets killed which is a blessing. I like to think that Rusty and Lucky insisted on no violence but who knows. The haul was not peanuts. Somebody said a million bucks which those days could have bought you a lot of top class motors and even a big garage to keep them nice and shiny.

The problem was it got complicated. Before the heist Rusty sneaks a visit to Lucky and tells him that psycho Santoro is planning to kill Lucky after the job. So after the stick up Lucky and Nicky Santoro are driving away to escape. The two others in the robbery are in another motor but Lucky and Santoro are in the auto with all the money and because Lucky does not want to drive to his death he thinks a detour might be in order. Lucky slugs Santoro and pushes him out of the pretend police car. That must have put a smile on the face of Lucky Jackson. Not the kind of smile that Lucky shared with his lady admirers but a smile I bet. Boom boom, indeed.

This is the way I heard the rest from folks in Vegas. So Lucky is driving the pretend police car and is on his way to meet Rusty who Lucky thinks still has the hots for him. Rusty is where she should be which would have put one of those famous smiles on the face of Lucky. But the problem is Rusty takes Lucky to a hotel where Nicky Santoro is ready, waiting and armed. Santoro plugs Lucky in the chest but somehow Lucky escapes. It didn't do him much good. Santoro hired a couple of hit men, and they found Lucky. These guys were professionals. Lucky was working in a blind school, teaching car repairs. That was the end of Lucky Jackson. The talk was that Lucky just stood there, as if he was waiting to die. We were close but I only ever knew him as Lucky. I'm not sure what they wrote on his tombstone but I'm damned sure it wasn't Lucky. People said Rusty really had the hots for Santoro but, after Lucky Jackson, I don't think so. Santoro had to have something on Rusty to make her sell out Lucky. What it was we'll never know. What I know is this, Rusty worked all her life and her and Lucky should have stayed together. Maybe that was why they argued so much. They needed one another and because of what was inside them they hated being that way. Rusty and Lucky had plenty of pride, that I remember. I used to think they were blessed. Cursed more like it.

LEW HARPER

HARPER/THE MOVING TARGET
USA 1966
DIRECTOR – JACK SMIGHT

I know that Lew Harper worked all over Los Angeles. He was a good man. We were friends. I did some work for him here in Reno and I was always willing. I would do the leg work, and my wife Phyllis used to check any local records. Sometimes I'd pop down to LA and we'd have a few beers and talk about what was wrong with the damned country.

He once said to me, Arnie, I'd like a job where death was not so close and grim.

I knew what Lew meant. I told him it could be worse. We could have worked in a mortuary. I can tell you that Lew Harper was straight, a good detective. He had these blue eyes that women liked but the man also had principles, too many for some. He wasn't popular, even with his blue eyes. Lew was too straight for the Long Beach Police Department. They fired him on some trumped up charge. Lew knew it was coming. His boss said something like there's always one, and you're it and you're fired. After that Lew went private. He slept in his office, and somehow kept his car on the road although you should have seen the state of the thing. The worst thing that happened to Lew Harper was Susan leaving. He never did get over her but, as Phyllis said to Lew on more than one occasion, he did not make it easy for the lady. The good news was that they didn't have kids. Lew didn't have to worry about that, just the rent on the office and keeping his motor on the road. Pity about Susan, though. She knew how to look after a man, and anyone with eyes in his head could tell you she was a good looking lady. In that way Lew was a fool.

It didn't help that he liked to have the last word. He was fine with Phyllis and me but his mouth too often got him into trouble. Lew worked in military intelligence in the war and that was where he met Albert Graves. Lew discovered that we all had secrets. Lew was too good at finding out what was behind the front door. It left him with a sour heart. He discovered there is more than death that is grim.

He used to say to me, Arnie, we all have to die.

I know that, I'd say.

So why can't we just behave ourselves in the stuff before?

That's the mystery, I'd say.

If Lew liked a drink, it didn't do him much harm. He kept his good looks and stayed in shape. Most of what he earned went on rent, the car and his suits for business. After that there wasn't that much money for booze.

I know that Lew Harper and Albert Graves are still friends. They've been pals since those days in the war. Albert understood. Lew had no option other than to tell the cops what he knew. Ralph Sampson was the guy that Albert killed. Ralph Sampson was loaded, a multi-millionaire when a million could buy you a Los Angeles boulevard. Albert was not long in prison. He had a smart lawyer that found as much dirt on Ralph Sampson as he could. After that no one on the jury was too worried about what had happened to Ralph Sampson or that his murderer was sitting in the middle of the courtroom.

Albert Graves was lucky. Knock off a millionaire and you expect the family to hire the best lawyer. But the Sampson family didn't give a damn. Ralph Sampson was not just cruel to his relatives, he liked to play the field. His wife and her stepdaughter detested Ralph Sampson almost as much as they hated each other. As far as they were concerned, Albert had done them a favour. The defence also had some tale about how Sampson had mistaken Albert for one of his kidnappers and attacked Albert. The smart lawyer claimed Albert was terrified and fired his gun to defend himself.

Sampson had been held up in this wrecked tanker by this doped up lady piano player, her brother and her boyfriend. The boyfriend of the doped up lady piano player was also hanging around Miranda, the daughter that hated Dad. Miranda had no idea who was behind the kidnapping. Lew had discovered where the kidnappers had hidden Sampson because the doped up lady piano player had confessed to Lew and had taken him to the wrecked tanker. When Lew went on the tanker looking for Sampson, the doped up lady piano player drove off in his car. His wife Susan may have found Lew impossible to live with but he could be gallant with women. This might be why Lew left the lady piano player behind in his car.

Lew had asked Albert to meet him at the tanker. Lew arrived, and there was no Albert and a dead Ralph Sampson. Lew got knocked out with a blow to the back of the head. I know because I felt the lump that was left. Albert appeared and woke up a drowsy Lew Harper. Like a good friend, Albert drove Lew home.

Lew could spot a liar a mile away. He figured that Albert was there before Lew arrived and Albert had killed Sampson. At one point Albert threatened Lew with a gun but they had seen too much together in the war. Albert dropped his gun and explained everything. This was how Lew knew that the courtroom story about Albert defending himself against Ralph Sampson was a load of hooey. Lew said nothing, though. He had handed Albert to the police and, as far as Lew was concerned, that was enough. He had stayed true to his principles. All in all Albert was lucky.

Lew Harper was not the vindictive kind. He liked to do his job and do the right thing. Lew Harper may have been a handsome man but he kept people at a distance. After Susan the women should have queued up in a line but they didn't. I know there were other casualties in the Sampson case. Alan Taggert, the boyfriend of the female piano player, was killed by Albert although Lew reckoned that Albert really did believe that Taggert at the time was going to kill Lew. I'm not so sure. I think Albert knew more about the kidnapping than he pretended. Miranda lost an unimpressive father and what she thought was a boyfriend. The step-mother was fine. She was glad to see the back of the cruel husband. Albert said he killed Ralph because when he saw him there inside the tanker he remembered all the cruelty and felt it had to end. Albert Graves also had the hots for Miranda, and there was no way Ralph Sampson would let that happen. How much of this is thought through before a killing, I don't know. I've never killed anyone. Maybe Albert just reacted, a lot just bubbled up inside him. Maybe Albert got used to life without Ralph Sampson and couldn't face him coming back.

Albert, though, was definitely serious over Miranda. Lew said she was a gorgeous dope but she was just a kid. After her father died, Miranda needed to get away from the wicked step-mother and Miranda meandered over to Italy. I discovered that Miranda met serious people. There must have been something in that Italian way of life that affected her. She cut off her gorgeous brunette locks, dyed the rest blonde and appeared in these serious Italian art movies. The last I heard Miranda was married to an academic philosopher. The news affected Lew, made him hate Los Angeles even more and how it stunted people. Lew could never leave, though.

I was built for this dung heap, he would say.

That was the difference. Miranda got out of LA while she was still young. Lew called her the one that got away.

People don't like to talk about it but in southern California over the years they've had problems with the Klan. Folks from Dixie came to work in the steel factories. Most were okay, and a lot of them were black but amongst the white folks a few were keen to establish Klan chapters. The LAPD didn't want to know about Klan persecution. The NAACP had to hire private help. Lew got involved. Lew was too young to do anything in '49 when O'Day Short and his family were killed. O'Day Short was a black activist who didn't like how housing estates in LA had to be either black or white.

The people in the Klan didn't like him not liking segregation and they bombed out him and his family. This stuff didn't end in '49. The Klan kept going away and coming back. Lew worked with the NAACP a few times. They liked him, and he enjoyed the work, more than digging his nose into the scandals of rich families, even if that paid well. Lew didn't like the rich. He called the rich the sour cream that rises to the top.

We had a small theatre in Reno. The actors were young people. They put on all kinds of weird stuff but it made a change from casinos and stupid cop movies. Lew was here for a weekend, and Phyllis and me dragged him to see this Greek thing called Oedipus. I'm not sure how but Lew got really interested in ancient Greek drama. He went to see all the plays, read books about it, but didn't talk much about what it all meant. He liked to keep it to himself. One night, though, I was in LA. I'd left Phyllis at home in Reno. Lew and me got together and sank a few beers.

I asked him, Lew, what's with all this Greek stuff?

He said he liked it. It helped him think about some of the cases he'd had to handle.

I see, I said, although I didn't.

I remember what followed.

Lew took a breath, sipped his beer, paused and said, Arnie, the cars get bigger but nothing changes.

I'd have said something but he just sat there and laughed.

WALKER

POINT BLANK
USA 1967
DIRECTOR – JOHN BOORMAN

I once asked Walker about his Christian name. He took a while to answer.

Well? I said.

You wouldn't like it, he said.

After that I always called him Walker, and he called me Millie because my name was Ann Miller. He could have called me Miller, of course, but Walker wasn't that kind of man. He liked a woman to look up to him. The truth is I'm a sucker for broken tough guys. I have a decent and reliable husband but Jim is anything but tough and the way he lives his life he isn't even bruised. Walker and me became close, and how it was at home there were no objections from Jim. I liked to spend a lot of time at the Lake, and Jim knew it. Walker liked to fish and after we met he liked to talk. That was what we did, just talked.

Walker arrived around 1970, and a couple of years before that The Kid had returned. The Kid grew up to be a different man from what we expected. Calling him The Kid has something to do with him not being able to hear or speak. The Kid that left Bridgeport had a sweet smile. The man that returned was still friendly but you mentioned Marney or what he'd been up to down in Los Angeles and a scowl would soon appear on his face. I didn't think The Kid had it in him but he must have had bad memories. I said all this to Walker one time.

We all have bad memories, said Walker.

And then he said something that surprised me. Walker wished he could remember more. He wasn't talking about forgetting things but not seeing the full picture, like imagining rooms without the furniture.

Too many memories are like dreams, said Walker.

When The Kid came home he bought back the garage he'd sold to pay for Marney and him to go and live in LA. The Kid had worked with Jeff Markham that time it all went wrong but that was over twenty years before The Kid returned and took over the garage again with the money he'd made in LA. This guy called Mal Grainger who had run this wire service in Los Angeles had given The Kid some money because he felt sorry for someone who was deaf and dumb. How much and where the rest of the money came from for the garage, I don't know.

Walker pumped petrol some days and did odd things around the place. At the lake where we met, Walker fished and chopped trees. By the time Walker appeared in Bridgeport we had a restaurant and not just the coffee shop Marney had left behind. The Kid had taken Marney to LA but he came back to Bridgeport without her. The tourists have increased over the years but most of them just pass through. Walker lived pretty well. He sold firewood and fish to the people in the town. Saturdays he would put a stall by the side of the highway. I would buy him a pack of cigarettes a couple of times a week.

I reckon I know just about everything about Walker. We talked a lot out there by the lake and we shared secrets. Walker knew about me and Jeff Markham which was why he felt he could tell me everything. Walker only robbed the payroll the syndicate dropped in Alcatraz because he had a friend that was in trouble.

Everybody thinks you're a vicious criminal, I said. They've heard awful tales.

Walker just grinned.

Most of that stuff is about this hoodlum called Parker, said Walker.

They confuse the names. Millie, believe me, I just did this one job in Alcatraz. It was a favour to my buddy, Mal.

Walker stopped talking and he stared at the lake for God knows how long. I remember that so well.

And? I said.

Mal tried to kill me. I thought he was my friend but he wasn't. I thought my wife loved me but she didn't.

The rest of that afternoon I let Walker talk. He put down his fishing rod, lit a cigarette and told me almost everything. I sat and listened and thought how I couldn't say any of this to Jim because he'd say I was only listening to Walker because I hadn't got over Jeff Markham. I hadn't and I never will but that wasn't why I spent time with Walker or not the only reason. I just thought Walker needed someone to listen to him. He talked a lot about his life as a marine and how it toughened him up which he said he liked a lot but it left him feeling empty which he didn't like at all. Walker liked a drink but I knew he had his reasons. We agreed that he had to stick to the beer which, all the time I knew him, he did.

Millie, he once said to me, guys like me have the armour on the inside. Walker was not long out of the Army when he met Mal. Walker, Mal and Lynne, that was the name of Walker's wife, they robbed the money in Alcatraz together. She must have been some tough lady, I thought. And then Walker told me the poor woman couldn't sleep nights and killed herself, and I didn't know what to think. I said to Walker that his wife must have known his first name when they married.

She didn't like it, either, said Walker.

The tale about Alcatraz and what Mal, Lynne and Walker did there chilled me but I'd had practice with Jeff Markham and I'd also spent too many afternoons thinking about Jeff and how he died. So I listened.

Alcatraz was bad, said Walker, but, Millie, so was the rest.

Because Mal wanted all the money for him and Lynne, he shot Walker in the stomach and left him for dead in Alcatraz. Walker was wearing a money belt. The money was not in it, Mal had all the money, but the belt and its buckle were thick enough to stop the bullets killing Walker. The next two days Walker recovered his strength and got himself clean in the sea. The ferry that took the tourists to Alcatraz arrived, and Walker sneaked a trip back to the mainland.

Walker wanted his share of the money that he had stolen with Mal and Lynne. But Mal had used most of the money to pay off his debt to these crooks that ran some criminal syndicate. I didn't understand why but these crooks accepted the money from Mal and gave him a well-paid job. The rest you can guess or at least half of it. Nobody wanted to pay Walker what he was owed. I never saw much of his stubborn side but I do know that he wouldn't bother with people who wanted him to knock down the price of his fish and firewood. He would just turn and walk away. Walker was honest with me. He left a trail of destruction, he said. I heard about the fights in detail. Walker had hurt people but apart from Mal he didn't kill anyone, and Mal was an accident.

I don't lose sleep over, Mal, said Walker. Lynne is different.

He showed me her pictures. She was a beautiful girl. Walker never did get the money he was owed although I was not sure why Walker felt the organisation owed him money because as far as I could see it was their money in the first place. That's right, Mal was robbing the people he owed. But Walker felt he was entitled. This man called Fairfax felt Walker deserved the money because the chaos Walker had caused meant that this man Fairfax was now in charge of everything and what was ninety three thousand dollars to a large criminal organisation that made money hand over fist. Walker and Fairfax went back to Alcatraz because, like before, money was still being left there by the syndicate. All ninety three thousand dollars were wrapped up and lying there on the floor of an empty prison and waiting to be picked up by Walker.

Millie, I just walked away, said Walker.

From the money? I said.

And then Walker lit a cigarette and stared at the lake. I waited until Walker finished his cigarette.

I don't regret it, Millie, he said. For a while I wondered if I was just spooked by the place, or by this guy Fairfax who'd got everything he wanted and held all the aces or this big bright light on the helicopter that dropped the money.

I waited while Walker played around with the line on his fishing rod. His messing must have lasted ten minutes. I didn't mind. I stared at the lake, and it was a sunny day. I thought about what he said and just what this guy Fairfax had been doing while Walker was fighting everyone. I had time.

Walker said, I don't know why I walked away but I don't regret not taking the money. And I think I knew at the time I wouldn't, knew that if I'd taken the money after everything happened, I'd have nothing left. You know what I mean, Millie?

That is the only time since I've known Walker that I imagined what it would have sounded like if Jeff had called me Millie.

Nothing left to live for? I said.

Walker smiled and said nothing but I knew I was right.

Walker never threw a punch, didn't even raise his voice with anyone here in Bridgeport. He would just walk away from trouble like he did when people didn't want to pay his price for his fish and firewood. I picture him at the side of the highway and sitting next to his fish and firewood stall and reading this book about King Arthur and Lancelot that he loved. I once bought him the famous book about King Arthur and the Holy Grail, the one written by the English guy called Mallory, but Walker couldn't settle with that. He liked the tale to be told in a simple way.

How many times have you read that book? I said.

It helps with the memories, said Walker.

I know there is or was a brutal man somewhere deep inside Walker but the man I knew was strong but lonely and the loneliness makes a difference. It can make a man gentle. Some men are just best when they are not around people or the wrong kind of women. Walker was like that. I was heartbroken when he died, he was carrying some lung disease that they have down there in Los Angeles. Occi or valley fever I think they call it. Walker never really talked about Fairfax. I think Fairfax gave Walker chills down his spine. All I know was that he was a Norwegian guy with a prominent Adam's Apple although Walker said he never noticed it.

STEVE SKORSKY

THEY CAME TO ROB LAS VEGAS
USA 1968
DIRECTOR – ANTONIO ISASI

What I wanted was to be a cop but the Treasury began recruiting Native Americans before the LAPD, so that was where I headed. My Cherokee roots are way back but I just about qualified. I also had an accountancy degree from UCLA. You can't argue with fate. They were good times. Back then in the '60s there were more jobs than people and gasoline was cheap. The inflation came later. I was urged to quit my job in the Treasury, and my friends said that I should move around. No regrets, I enjoyed the work and had a career. I had good people around me and, people don't understand this, I could take risks. I was a Civil Servant and I worked in a job that had excitement. That day when the Skorsky truck blew up out of the desert and money and gold went up in the sky and everywhere, hot damn, the memory still puts a smile on my face. Even Tony Vincenzo, the guy who did the heist, went in the police wagon and laughed all his way to jail. I've never seen a man look so miserable as Steve Skorsky did that day. After his spell in the penitentiary, Tony Vincenzo disappeared from sight. I hope the man was all right, even if the robbery he pulled had made my job difficult. I'll be honest. Tony Vincenzo had me pulling my hair out which I shouldn't because I have good Cherokee hair. His brother thought Tony was some kind of hippie but burying that armoured truck under the desert was hard work. And the one thing hippies didn't like was physical effort.

I put my career on the line with Steve Skorsky. It went down to the last call, the trip where the armoured truck exploded out from under the desert. If we hadn't nailed Skorsky then, I was off the case.

What a sight. Before all that I had eased my way into the Storsky Corporation. After he found out I was a Treasury employee, Storsky called me a fake and a fink. I was both yet I enjoyed it, walking around Skorsky Security as if I were the insurance expert that his company needed. And I even liked the man. His employees liked him, and he had Native Americans, Mexicans, Afro-Americans and women on the payroll long before it was mandatory. Storsky paid his people decent wages. He two-timed his wife, of course, but with a secretary like Ann Bennett the men that would have resisted her would have been few.

What happened to Steve Skorsky was terrible. But you don't cross the Mob and guys like Salvatore. I know from experience. After we collected the haul from the exploded armoured truck I had a couple of telephone calls telling me that something was going to happen to my family. My team rounded up Salvatore and a few of his henchmen. We all had a good long conversation. I mentioned that the United States Government did not take kindly to its officials being intimidated by hoods. I said we either let bygones be bygones or the Government would close down Vegas. It couldn't have, of course, but a lot of damage could have been done to their gambling business. I had the support of this FBI guy called Dave Bannion. He was a big help. Not only did the Mob take him seriously, he was an ex-cop that had stood up to gangsters in LA. Dave was good at getting the local police to play ball. Right from the start I had office space in the police department. I also had desks in Skorsky Corporation and the insurance company Storsky employed. I was never at my own desk. They were good times.

The problem had been that this crook Salvatore had Skorsky smuggling gold out of the country. Steve Storsky wanted out of the deal but Salvatore had the poor guy in his grip. Skorsky Corporation was the best security company in the business. Their trucks were built like tanks, and they used a computer monitoring system that would have helped a rocket ship to find the moon. All that, though, cost money, and the money to pay for it Skorsky had raised through not very nice people. They expected lifetime loyalty. I believed Storsky when he said he had told the Mob that this was the last trip he would smuggle gold. The man was making enough money running cash and bail bonds for the banks and legitimate companies. Skorsky would have had more luck if he had stuck to the crooked but with all those computers he needed to employ regular people. Mixed in with them were the crooks that filtered the gold trips into the regular runs. That was how we knew which runs carried the contraband. Skorsky always had to use the same three deadbeat security guards to smuggle the gold.

Tony Vincenzo had a big grudge against Steve Skorsky. His older brother Gino was killed when he had tried to rob a Skorsky haul. There were a few years between Tony and Gino. Tony realised that his brother and the other old guys were past their prime. Between the security guards, defence systems on the truck that fired unforgiving bullets and the police that were on the scene in minutes, Gino and his friends had no chance. Not one survived. Tony pledged revenge and he succeeded. Skorsky lost his biggest haul and perhaps the one where Skorsky wanted to say quits, like he said. Hiding the truck under the desert was a cute trick but Tony and his men had to work on the truck and under the desert for four days. Tempers frayed, and there were arguments. Tony told me all about it. He had this pothead called Cooper, this impatient guy that not only blew up the truck, dollars and gold but the body parts that held Mr Cooper together. Collecting all of him for a body bag was not so pleasant.

Tony had worked right there in Vegas. He was a croupier on a blackjack table. Tony was good with cards, and he could spot cheats and card counters. He did a few card tricks for me. Tony was good fun. The casino owners in Vegas liked him. He should have stuck to the cards but Tony had that grudge. I asked him where and how he learnt the card tricks. Tony mentioned this guy called Sydney. Tony said that Sydney was not much older than him and a few inches shorter but he acted like a father to him. I met Sydney a couple of times. Sydney told me about working in this motel in LA in the '40s where he reckoned that the Black Dahlia killing had happened. I pretended to be interested. He was a wise guy but very polite. We talked about Tony but, if he knew anything, Sydney was not for telling. Sydney moved later to Reno. I do hope the Mob didn't find Tony after he came out of the penitentiary. Maybe Sydney helped Tony to slip out of sight. Tony did a long stretch inside. He lost his good looks behind bars. But what happened to the man he robbed was much worse. What poor Skorsky suffered was terrible.

Even though the exploding truck ruined his business and he had spent time inside prison, Steve Skorsky was working and earning good money when the Mob found him. He had too much knowledge of the business not to be valuable to security firms. His wife had left him while he was inside. I found her to be friendly. Of course, she looked nothing like Ann Bennett. Without a wife to ask him where he'd been, Skorsky spent on the hookers too much of what he earned but, if you want to do that, there is no better place than Vegas. In his own way Steve Skorsky also had a grudge because Tony Vincenzo had known what was happening inside the Skorsky company, and more important which truck carried what where. Skorsky's secretary, Ann Bennett, had also been hopping into bed with Tony Vincenzo. Skorsky had treated Ann like a queen, and because of her he lost his business and went to prison. After something like that happens to a man the hookers in Vegas can be very tempting.

Skorsky was with a hooker when Salvatore found him. They dragged Skorsky and the hooker out to Death Valley and buried the poor guy in the desert and up to his head in sand. The hooker was hysterical, and I heard that Salvatore and the others slapped her around. They may have done other things. If they did, Skorsky would have had to watch. The Mob has a strong sense of poetic justice. The truck of Skorsky had been buried under the ground and exploded, so why not do the same to Steve Skorsky, thought Salvatore. Just when Skorsky thought the only thing he needed was a drop of water, a moment's respite perhaps, Salvatore bent down and put a stick of dynamite into the mouth of Skorsky. Salvatore lit the fuse, and Skorsky, whose arms and legs were trapped under the desert, watched the fuse burn all the way down to his mouth. The agony ended when his head was blown off his shoulders. I suppose having the hooker along added to the humiliation. She was the only one watching that was not smoking a cigar. The cigars were for comic effect I was told. Salvatore was convicted for the crime but not until years later when FBI man Dave Bannion recruited a Mob informer who told the tale and all its gory details. I haven't seen Dave Bannion since he retired. I did hear that he was doing some investigatory work for a writer who had this theory about the Black Dahlia murder. I wonder if Bannion ever talked to Sydney.

ANDY KILVINSKI

THE NEW CENTURIONS
USA 1972
DIRECTOR – RICHARD FLEISCHER

1972 was a bad year for the LAPD, not as bad as '65 when we had the Watts riots but not good. Most years LA simmers, and even when it doesn't I have a lot more to worry about than the suicide of a retired cop that walked the beat all his life. But whatever the heat, my secretary cleared the diary and I attended the funeral of Andy Kilvinski. The guy had a decent turnout which is one of the benefits of being employed by the LAPD, I suppose, lots of uniforms and plenty of people. There was a good number at the funeral of my father Lieutenant Preston Exley, and when I take my final look at the ceiling I expect the Mayor will look at his diary. They will all be there even if most of them hate the guts of Police Commissioner Ed Exley.

My secretary may make suggestions about funerals but I decide. I was at the funeral for Kilvinski because a suicide is what the men talk about. The rookie cops look up to the old timers, and we lose enough new recruits as it is. Later, when they are tied into the pension, it's different. After Kilvinski died I needed to make a statement for all the cops that walk the beat, and me being at the funeral was that statement. Suicide in the LAPD is unusual. The typical cop retires on a good nest egg. The USA has over half a million cops. Each year about two hundred of them commit suicide, and just over a hundred are killed in the line of duty. LAPD has a good record for the low number of suicides amongst its cops. I don't want any suicides but I would rather be below the average than above.

One of the first things I ever did was set up a programme to minimise the incidence of suicide. My enemies said I was just covering my back. Maybe I was but the programme did no harm. We put all our cops on a one-day course. We did surveys of our cops on how they felt privately. The surveys were anonymous so that the replies would be honest. Some of the opinions we read were hard to take but I just stuck my chin out. I believe I'm good at that. Every cop left the one-day course with a leaflet and a dashboard sticker that had two words KNOW SUICIDE in bold red letters. LAPD averages about two a year. Considering LAPD has nearly 10,000 cops that is not bad. Don't ever get a transfer to Chicago. I don't know what goes on up in the windy city but a Chicago cop on the beat is five times more likely to chop himself than a cop not walking the streets.

Klivinski killed himself after he retired. That was unusual. Most suicides happen to cops who've been in the force for twenty years or more and are still serving officers. Suicide is an old man's disease. Well, the experts have an explanation. They call it emotional isolation. I think in simpler terms. One day you're a tough guy, and the next you're an eggshell. Have I been there? I've known stress and I've felt shaky but the eggshell? I could always see it coming but then I had advantages. My father was a cop, a good cop, and that helped. I am smarter than the average member of the LAPD or smart enough to have an education. More important than being smart is wanting to be smart.

What goes wrong with the cops who commit suicide? This is my theory. I'll tell you a tale. I was once taken to dinner by this top journalist. I should remember his name but I can't. This journalist was doing a piece on racism in the LAPD, the usual. I asked him how he faced a typewriter each morning and how did he know when his articles were finished. I told him, when Ed Exley wrote anything, some report, anything, I would read it and read it again and keep finding faults. This journalist said you have to do your best and enjoy taking pride in what you do, it is how you earn your living. And if it goes well, you will do it as well as the others. But at the same time, this journalist said, you have to have contempt for what you do. There will always be another day, another journalist, something else to write and readers who will remember damn all of what you have written.

If you take it too seriously, said this journalist, you won't get anywhere.

It made sense to me. I am Los Angeles Police Commissioner Edward Exley. I realised a long time ago I would never make the streets safe for the good citizens of LA. I doubt I ever wanted to. Do not rely on Ed Exley to extinguish evil or even hold the line, whatever that means. I hear police on the streets say that all the time. If the line will eventually snap, so be it. What I will do is my job as well as most of the other police commissioners out there.

I do not want to be unkind to cops like Andy Kilvinski but the cop on the beat is the lowest grade within the LAPD. Think about how I do my job as police commissioner. I'm not stupid. I understand that there will always be cops doing and saying things that go against everything I preach. I go to sleep every night knowing something is happening on the streets that denies what I have promised the citizens of Los Angeles. The point is this, if you can't go to sleep knowing that you have a group of people in the workforce that compromise and betray you on a daily basis then you shouldn't be a police commissioner.

Too many cops on the beat can't think this through. They use cynicism to survive but what a cop really needs is cold hearted pragmatism. The cold heart may make you indifferent to people and human suffering but it gives you space to make a difference. And that in the long run might just help people a little. Cynicism just makes you brood on what is the point. You do not climb the ranks of an American police force without knowing that the paradox is where human beings came in. Maybe that should be the other way round. Either way you should get my point. An old cop that has pounded the beat for twenty years has survived and endured. Most of the time he has been lording it over someone, the wrecks on the street, the endless supply of rookies and the cops that resign and move on.

Not everyone that resigns is disillusioned about the work or loses sleep because they can't see how they will win the battle against evil or hold the damned line the old timers go on about. An awful lot see the job as a stepping stone to qualifying as a lawyer. The best cops become detectives and administrators and have careers, the next best become lawyers, and the rest stay on the beat. Guess who the beat cops hate the most and look down their noses at? That's right everyone who isn't walking the beat. Me and people like me, the beat cops think we're overpaid failures. Kilvinski endured, and I don't underestimate what that entailed, patrolling the streets every day, but the man was never going to be a first grade cop. He was limited to walking the beat and, if he were like the typical cop on the beat, he wouldn't have done it very well. An underpaid hero perhaps but also a hopeless failure. When Kilvinski retired the adrenaline the job gave him dried up. Kilvinski forgot the authority he'd had on the streets and remembered the failure. If he'd stayed married, it might have been different.

Rookies come into the force and they're impressed with the old guys. The rookies confuse experience with competence and assume endurance alone amounts to heroism. Maybe the guys pounding the beat should be remembered as heroes. I wouldn't like to have walked the streets for twenty years but we need to understand that while heroes may help you in crucial moments those same heroes have limitations. Don't talk to them about plans and progress. I've stuck my neck out, and there were times when it required what felt to me like courage but I never thought it made me a hero. The problem with these guys is that they either go back to sweet wives who worry about them and want just that their heroes come home safe or, like Kilvinski, they have no one. I can't remember my wife Inez ever being sweet with me. Knowing you're living with someone who doesn't give a damn whether you come home or not helped me. How? It fortified my contempt.

I understand that the mind of Kilvinski was not working properly but I didn't like the way the man killed himself, blowing his brains out like that and in the middle of his own living room. Another copper would have had to clear up the mess, probably one of the adoring rookies. Kilvinski should have thought it through. For two years after Kilvinski put the pistol inside his mouth and killed himself the LAPD recorded no suicides at all. The Know Suicide campaign helped but it helped that the other cops knew Kilvinski went out the way he did. So maybe the guy did us and his adoring rookies a favour. I met his daughter and granddaughter at the funeral. That was the only family the poor guy had. The ex-wife didn't make an appearance. I'm not even sure that the woman is in Los Angeles. I shook hands with the daughter and granddaughter but that was about it. They looked more Polish than Kilvinski did. His daughter and granddaughter would have been given what Kilvinski left behind but you don't expect a police badge to mean that much to a young girl. The granddaughter cried a lot, more than her mother. No, I don't remember the names of the family. I imagine it was not Kilvinski. I assumed his daughter was married, seeing as she had a child. I should have asked what their names were but I didn't.

CARL KOLCHAK

THE NIGHT STALKER
USA 1972
DIRECTOR – JOHN LLEWELLYN MOXEY

Will I ever forget Carl Kochak? Absolutely no way, I promise that. I was close to the man, always close. Some of the local cops in Vegas didn't approve of pressmen poking their noses into police investigations but they had their heads in the sand. Most of those news guys had learnt their trade in Los Angeles, and out there they have a tradition of reporters digging into criminal cases to try and solve them. The newsboys do it to sell papers. Not everyone is the same but I liked working in Las Vegas, the whole time. I never gambled which is how it should be if you work for the FBI in Vegas. Should be doesn't mean it is. My only weakness was that the first chance I got I used to meet people at the side of pools in the big hotels. I would sit there in the sun, watch the ladies walk by, have a beer and collect what information was around. What those waitresses wore those days. You wouldn't get away with it today, not even in Vegas.

I was fifty when Janus Skorzeny arrived in town. I should have been past thinking about the waitresses in short skirts but when I told those ladies I was an FBI agent it did no harm. Once in a while an odd young thing would get friendly, enough for my smiles to be worth it. I stayed in the FBI right until the end. I had three reasons, Dave Bannion, the pension and where I worked. Dave was a couple of years ahead of me but he had been around the block, had some important scalps both in LA and here in Vegas, and I thought of him as an old timer. Dave showed me the ropes. After that and a few smiles from the poolside bikini babes I was convinced the FBI and Vegas was the life for me.

Carl Kolchak was not an ex-Los Angeles man like most of us. He started out in New York but, because he had a habit of falling out with people about how his stories should read, he'd been obliged to chase jobs around the country. Kolchak thought Vegas was strictly backyard which was another reason he had more time for his own opinions than those inside the heads of the local enforcement officers. I didn't mind that. At least he listened to me. I liked the way Kolchak had to go around butting his head against everything and everyone. I'm not that kind of guy or that kind of FBI man but Kolchak had a sense of humour, and the guys who have to barge in are not only useful, they make life interesting. Kolchak had that fast way of talking they have up there in New York. If Dave Bannion ever had a sense of humour, it passed me by but in an odd way Kolchak reminded me of Dave. They believed in themselves and in what they were doing. Not enough people, especially these days, have a sense of right and wrong.

The local cops patronised Kolchak. They'd let him talk and then walk out the room as if he hadn't been there. It hurt the guy. Kolchak wasn't as tough as he pretended. But after the Skorzeny business they took Kolchak seriously, too seriously perhaps, considering the way they treated him, although something had to be done. You can't leave dead guys around with stakes sticking out their chests even if they've been walking the streets as if they're vampires. Looking back I think we all got carried away. Janus Skorzeny was a tough guy and more than a match for the local cops. One-handed he threw a guy out of a hospital window. The stuff about it being one-handed is true. Kolchak claimed that the cops shot Skorzeny in the chest and it had no effect. I don't believe it. Most of those LA beat cops couldn't hit a barn door. Kolchak was seeing the story he wanted to write. He got carried away but then we all did.

No doubt Janus Skorzeny believed he was a vampire. He bit the necks of his victims, drained their blood, stole bottles of the stuff from the hospital and even had a woman hostage tied up in

CARL KOLCHAK

his home so he could drain a few drops for his nightly nightcap. Kolchak had this kooky girlfriend, Gail something. She was a bit younger than Carl but he was a newsman. He knew how to make her laugh and had stories to tell. Gail had lived in a hippy commune before coming to Vegas, and I reckoned she still smoked pot. Gail was convinced that Skorzeny was a bona fide vampire. Gail had all these weird books. I don't think Kolchak was partial to the special weed but he did listen to her. More important, Kolchak was always chasing the story of a lifetime, you know, something to nail his ticket back to the Big Apple. I wasn't sure Gail was the right girl for Kolchak but what happened, the way the Vegas cops hounded her out of town so that they could do the same to Kolchak, brother, that was tough. Dave Bannion was never number one when it came to the rights of suspects and so on but even Dave thought that what they did to Gail was out of line.

But if the cops were out of line, and I didn't like the way I was told to look the other way when it happened, then Kolchak also crossed the line. You don't put a stake through the heart of anyone, even if he has killed four women and has got a fifth tied to a bed with a transfusion unit strapped to her neck. The deal offered to Kolchak was simple. They wouldn't prosecute him for killing Skorzeny but he had to keep dumb and leave Vegas. They forgave him but just this once. I felt sorry for Carl but the Vegas cops kind of had a point. Kolchak had not only killed Skorzeny but driven a stake through the heart of the dead man. They were right to not prosecute but also right to worry about being held up to ridicule for stepping aside. Not everyone wanted Kolchak to walk away free. I had to remind people of the four women Skorzeny had murdered and the poor dame that Skorzeny had pinned to the bed. If we hadn't found Shelley Forbes in the house, it would have been much different for Kolchak. Without Forbes, the woman he rescued, Kolchak would have been charged with murder.

In a way the worst thing the Vegas cops did was give Kolchak a break. It convinced him that Skorzeny really was a vampire and the story was being buried for that reason. No one wanted the story to come out, that's true, but not because they believed Skorzeny was an immortal vampire. Vegas is a tourist spot. It was difficult enough back then keeping the wise guys in the background. That was my main job. I didn't need to worry about chasing vampires. What the cops were afraid of was not a plague of vampires but tourists staying away, period.

I will never blame Kolchak for putting the stake through the heart of Skorzeny. The guy had given us the runaround. If he hadn't been distracted by the sunlight coming through the window, we'd never have got him down on the floor. I understand Kolchak getting carried away because for a couple of days so was yours truly. That was why I watched Kolchak hammer in the stake and said nothing. The problem was that Kolchak stayed carried away. If anything, he got worse. I had this FBI file that claimed Skorzeny had been born in 1899. Kolchak said it proved Skorzeny was a vampire even though later I found out that the file was a joke played by one of the guys back in the office. Kolchak was like that, though. Once he had an idea in his head he wouldn't let it go.

I said to him, If Skorzeny was a genuine vampire, why weren't his victims walking around Vegas sinking their teeth into the necks of the tourists?

The women have been cremated, said Kolchak.

He slapped his knee as he said it. He was right but before they became crisp cinders the ladies had plenty of time to walk free out of the mortuary. Well, they didn't.

Kolchak has survived is what I know. He even linked up with Tony Vincenzo, his newspaper boss in Vegas. They moved to Seattle and then right across the country to Chicago. After a while Carl had a reputation and they put him on any story that had spooky legs. He never saw Gail again, which I knew hurt him. He used a lot of his money putting adverts in the papers but she never responded. Maybe she went back to some commune. I felt sorry for Carl. His editors should have put him on organised crime. He could have made a difference. Either that or have wasted years like me fighting a crooked system. You know, you have a lovely smile. How old are you? You look younger.

DETECTIVE MIKE KENEELY AND DETECTIVE PATRICK FARRELL

BUSTING
USA 1974
DIRECTOR – PETER HYAMS

You'll have to excuse me. This is the time for my mid-morning tablet. I have eight of these beauties every day. Eight tablets and no swearing, doctor's orders. Thanks for the water. If you think that's depressing, you should see what I'm eating for lunch. Still, if it keeps me out of hospital. Although the hospitals in LA have been good to me, I have to say. You want to know how often we tried peddling cocaine from my hospital bed? Ten times. You have to try different things. Keneely and the little guy he called a partner got wise, and that was the end of the hospital scam. It didn't make much difference. I was running out of hospitals to use and I have a heart condition. As Johnny Rosselli used to say to me, you have to look after the people who look after you. Johnny Rosselli, there was a wise guy that had style.

Let's get this straight. There was no big chase with me in one ambulance and Keneely and the little guy in another. I stepped outside the hospital. That was all. I walked into the hospital grounds because those two guys carried chaos around with them. I was protecting the hospital, you could say. I stood outside, smoked a cigarette and waited for the two dopes to come out and arrest me. I knew there'd be no conviction. We were moving cocaine in and out of my hospital room but they couldn't prove I touched the stuff. The cocaine was carried in flowerpots. In it came and out it went.

Not the best way to move cocaine or anything for that matter but in my business you have to try different things.

I didn't like either of them. They were a pair of, no, I mustn't swear. The doctor wants me to learn to be calm. What was the name of the little guy? That's right, Patrick Farrell. They didn't look Irish to me. Keneely and Farrell, who would have thought. Some of my buddies are Irish, and every one of them looks as if someone in the family was Irish. No way did Keneely and Farrell look Irish to me. I know Farrell had a Mexican mother, so okay. And I heard about Keneely and the trouble he had with his folks but where they were from I never heard. You have to understand. If you're in my kind of business, you expect heat. Here in LA we have a history of cops that like to push around guys like me. It goes right back to Commissioner Bill Parker and his Gangster Squad. The LAPD don't know any better which is why guys like me have to be philosophical. I paid good money to the LAPD. All I asked was that I could do what I did like any businessman. That was the deal. If I stepped out of line, used too much muscle, then fair enough, I'd live with the consequences. But I don't want heat for day to day business, no way is that right.

I haven't a clue why Keneely and the little guy acted the way they did. They knew about the money I paid the LAPD. And we're not talking about small potatoes. You don't hand over that kind of cash so two guys can play at being Wild Bill Hickok and Wyatt Earp on the streets of LA. Me, I blame the crime shows. The cops watch too many movies. And we had strange times back then in the '70s. They let these cops grow their hair, talk out the side of their mouths and walk around as if they were kings of the streets. The world has settled down. People are more reasonable these days. You get more support for the businessman. That's a good thing, don't you think?

Keneely had a problem with his old man, so I heard. The old guy liked a drink, I heard, and slapped his family around. Keneely wanted to sort out men like his father and hated authority,

DETECTIVE MIKE KENEELY AND
DETECTIVE PATRICK FARRELL

so I was told. The little guy, what was his name? That's right, Patrick Farrell. He just didn't like cops. Something happened between his Mexican mother and one of the cops out there in Hollinbeck. Something that didn't make the woman have high opinions of white folks. This happened just after Farrell had become a cop. After that he talked about leaving LAPD but never did. From what I heard, Farrell talked about leaving all of the time but his mother wanted him to hold out for the pension or something. He walked around with a cigarette in his mouth but didn't smoke. The cigarette wasn't lit. I suppose it helped him stay off the nicotine. How many cigarettes he got through, I don't know. He must have had more than one. I used to give out Havana cigars to the LAPD. People forget these things.

They were both oddballs. Keneely, though, was different. He had the guts to quit. Resigning from the LAPD was the first thing he did when I was acquitted after the hospital bust. I didn't know at the time. He just walked out of the court. I didn't even get time to laugh in his face which I would have done if I'd had the chance. Keneely hasn't done much since, so I heard. Someone put him on a training course, and he finished up as a crime scene investigator. You know the kind of thing. He'd walk around the crime scene and take photos, samples and stuff. If it helped him switch off from getting heated up about guys like me then good luck to the man because he didn't definitely switch off about me as far as I could see. I'll be honest. I think a lot of it was envy. You know, these two cops see me with a fine family, a big house, fancy cars and a few flunkeys. If Keneely and Farrell didn't hate me, they'd have to hate themselves. As Johnny Rosselli told me when I was still a kid, don't envy no one, just count the dollars and cents.

The one time I was out of order with those guys. One time, that's all. I arranged that they got a beating, a black guy who had his own issues with the LAPD. I knew I'd get my money's worth. Listen, the rackets are like any business. Sometimes you have to lay the law down but no one goes places by being a pain in the butt all the time. Someone has to like you. You understand what I mean? Johnny Rosselli had Jack Dragna. Mickey Cohen had Bugsy Seigel. Bugsy had Meyer Lansky. Being polite is important, having respect for others. A smile and a handshake don't take no more than a second. I'm courteous. All those guys in the rackets knew how to be polite. But sometimes you have to draw a line. And that was the way it was with Keneely and Farrell. I was paying good money to the LAPD. Keneely and Farrell thought they were above the law. Least that's how I see it.

I can be short tempered. I admit it, eight tablets and no swearing is where my temper got me. When I look at guys like Jimmy Fratianno and, rest in peace, Frank Bompensiero, I know I didn't have their patience. Those guys had the FBI on their backs all their lives but they didn't react. But now I think about it, that's the point. That's what the FBI does. It persecutes guys like Frank, Jimmy and me. We know it and live with it. But two small time LAPD vice-cops with Irish names who don't even look Irish throwing their weight about. That wasn't right and it isn't. Look, I don't want to be the main man. I remember what Johnny Rosselli told me when I was out in Vegas one time.

Carl, he said, you enjoy the good life. You don't throw it away by wanting to be number one.

You think? I said.

It ain't worth it, said Johnny.

He was right. I worry about my family and the dollars and cents. That's the advice I give to anyone. Worry about the dollars and cents and if you're going to play around, stick to the professionals. Excepting the lady at home the nearest I've got to nice girls are strippers. And I'm still here and married. I have a fine house, my two kids are doing well in college and they have a loving mother and father. I thank Johnny Rosselli for that.

Listen, I have no grievance against the LAPD. They played by the rules and did what they could to get Keneely and Farrell back into line. But putting those guys on the worst vice jobs like they did only made it worse. Keneely and Farrell got into fights trying to make arrests in gay bars because that will happen and because those people think like the rest of us. The gays always thought they had rights. I say live and let live and the gay porn pays the same as the rest. Sitting in a toilet all day waiting to catch a cheapskate cruiser is no job for anyone, especially Keneely and Farrell who thought they were Wild Bill Hickok and Wyatt Earp. But something would have nagged away at anyone doing that five days a week.

I can tell you what it was that they brooded about waiting in the toilets in the parks, me, Carl Rizzo. It twisted them. The more they thought about me the more they must have thought my life was perfect. Well it wasn't and it isn't. I'm a guy that had a smile and handshake for everyone and only ever worried about the dollars and cents but just look at what happened. Here I am and talking to you two guys who are telling me I'll have nothing to worry about once I'm in the witness protection programme. You FBI guys have patience, I'll give you that, listening to me talk about two crazy cops when what you really want to know is who ordered the hit on Frank 'The Bomp' Bompensiero. Who bumped The Bomp eh? And after what happened to The Bomp, you think I'm going to tell you? Screw you, no, Mister, that ain't swearing.

ROB CAULFIELD

NARROW MARGIN
USA 1990
DIRECTOR – PETER HYAMS

Because you are here, I had the DA's office send me the Leo Watts file. I have to return it tomorrow. If my old firm is letting an old retired DA take out files, I could not have been so bad, you think? Not that I expect to ever convince Rob Caulfield of my merit. That last year he worked as Deputy DA, Rob spent most of it believing I was on the payroll of Leo Watts. I was the Chief District Attorney. A man in my position expects some loyalty.

I told him, Rob, you watch too many movies.

Dahlbeck was the lawyer that this gangster Leo Watts had in his pocket. You've guessed it. I can see by the look on your face. Rob rang Dahlbeck and urged him not to say anything to me about Leo Watts. Of course, I can understand why Rob didn't suspect Dahlbeck. I see no shame in being serious about a career, and Dahlbeck was a clean cut and enthusiastic career man, so we thought. It turned out that Dahlbeck was even more ambitious than we realised.

I'd like to say that after the success with the Leo Watts case the relationship I had with Rob Caulfield improved and we became friends. But Rob was not the type to eat humble pie and I am not the best at accepting apologies. Rob thought the case against Leo Watts was open and shut because he had Carol Hunnicut as a witness to Leo killing Michael Tarlow. I understood we had enough to proceed but I told Rob not to make any assumptions about what might happen. For a while in court it was touch and go. Hunnicut wobbled a little when the defence attorney put on the pressure but fortunately for us the woman was classy and gorgeous.

The jury was hardheaded enough to convict a known criminal but not so unforgiving that they were not impressed by Hunnicut. She was lovely although she was not pleased when I suggested we have someone advise her what to wear in court. Rob loved seeing Hunnicut take me down a peg.

We are both old men now and no doubt he has mellowed as much as I have but sensibly we keep our distance. I did, though, attend his book launch but I was the only one from the DA's office, and that says something. I may not have liked Rob Caulfield but I was pleased for the man. Of course, Rob reckoned I was only there because of my responsibilities as Chief District Attorney, that me being there had nothing to do with friendship. Rob was half right. I had no affection and my respect, although it existed, was muted by too many bruises. Carol Hunnicut was at the book launch. She worked in publishing and helped Rob with the book. Hunnicut and Rob stayed friendly after the Leo Watts case. He saved her life which I suppose always helps, and she gave him a triumph with which he could end his legal career. Note my words. Rob Caulfield wanted more than earning a living and having a career. He wanted to triumph. Being victorious was how Rob Caulfield defined success. In our work that adolescent attitude can provide the occasional benefit but, believe me, over time it becomes wearing. I know Rob was fond of the son of Carol Hunnicut. But Rob Caulfield and Hunnicut were close friends and nothing more.

Rob was always more friendly with the LAPD detectives than the other attorneys. Rob had been a marine in Vietnam and whatever he left of himself over there in that disaster it was not his ego. He must have wrapped it up in his kit bag. Wherever Rob had worked after his Army stint he would have walked around believing his job was the most difficult and most important, the most demanding in the organisation. You know this kind of man, I am sure. Every workplace has one. Rob Caulfield wore his integrity on his sleeve, and most of us found it a little irritating. He retired as Deputy District Attorney and, of course, everybody would always ask me why because Rob had been top in his class at law school and in the Marines he had earned enough medals to be considered a leader of men. Well, taking men into battle isn't quite the same as keeping lawyers motivated through the daily drudge of one criminal case after another with not much in the way of returns.

Rob Caulfield resented my authority and that meant he disliked me. But he was happy to see me at the book launch. We had some memories, I suppose. His enmity had nothing to do with me being a black man and him white. If it had, I would not have been at his book launch. Our mutual antagonism was between equals. I forgot, I was saying. Rob was more friendly with the LAPD detectives than the other attorneys. After he retired, Rob needed an interest, and a few detectives and Rob used to meet every other Friday and talk about the old times. They had a back room in some restaurant where they ate, drank and talked. Mere chat, though, was not enough for hero Rob Caulfield. He was a fit sixty year old when he retired, and his nature was such that he would struggle to settle into old age. Rob kept in touch with Hunnicut but there were seventeen years between them and Rob was not handsome. I heard, though, that some women liked him because he was big, healthy and fit. He also had this young man's smile that he would use to get his way. The smile would appeal to a woman but, personally, I expect more than mechanical self-effacing innocence from my colleagues.

Rob had no real family. The detectives at the back of the restaurant were the same as Rob, lonely men disconnected from the families they had half started. Meeting once a fortnight with men like themselves to talk, eat good food and leave drunk was all they had. I was saying. I forgot again. Mere chat was not enough for hero Rob Caulfield. He suggested that rather than merely remember old times they should work their way through the unsolved cases. And this is what they did. This would have appealed to Rob because it would have allowed him to complain about me and what happened in my office.

At some point failed court cases led to talk about unsolved mysteries. Maybe the other detectives were bored of listening to Rob gripe about me. All the unsolved crimes they discussed were from Los Angeles and, inevitably, one dominated the rest. No, I am not even going to let you guess. Rob Caulfield is not the only person to write a book about the murder of Elizabeth Short but, credit where it is due, his was one of the best. The detectives from the back room of the restaurant helped him with the research, and Rob recruited an ex-FBI man that had once worked for the LAPD. The guy was called Dave Bannion, and his job was to evaluate and weigh the research of the detectives. This guy Bannion was really old and he lasted only a couple of years but Rob gave him a big write up in the book. Not that Rob needed help. He knew how to challenge assumptions made by policemen. Rob should have. I spent enough time showing him how. Carol Hunnicut helped with the book. I already knew from his legal work that Rob Caulfield was a capable writer. Carol found the publishing company and the market. The book was not a flop but no big hit either.

I heard Rob talking about the book on a few radio interviews. Most were here in LA but once he even travelled to New York to appear on some big radio station. The book didn't earn him enough money to change how he lived in retirement but that wouldn't have bothered Rob Caulfield. What he needed was more important than what money buys. Rob named the murderer or at least the man that Rob thought killed Elizabeth Short. A few suspects have been named over the years. Rob chose Dr George Hill Hodel. It is possible. Right now Hodel is the popular choice. As a DA, you survive by not being particular about convictions, what is important is nailing the criminal for something. Dr George Hill Hodel may not have killed Elizabeth Short but there are too many accusations about his misdemeanours for him to not have killed someone. If people believe Hodel killed Elizabeth Short, he cannot complain. Dr George Hill Hodel was a bad man. He threw these bizarre sex parties in which some of the girls were hurt.

Hodel was twisted enough to finish his after dinner conversations by watching movies of postmortems. I know, a barrel of laughs. In the DA's office the belief is that Hodel raped his daughter and killed his secretary. A couple of his relatives attended the book launch. I expected trouble but they were fine. Hodel may not be the Black Dahlia killer but his family realised, like I said, that whatever the accusations Dr George Hill Hodel could have no complaints.

I certainly give credit to Rob for what happened on that train with Carol. The man saved her life. We found the bodies of the two men on the train who were trying to kill Hunnicut. Somehow Rob fought them off. It is not impossible. Rob was a big healthy man who understood combat. The railway security guard paid with his life for what happened, so he must have done something to help. Do I believe that Rob fought to the death with a hit woman on top of a train while demure Carol Hunnicut was at his side hanging on to the roof? Come on. The body of the supposed hit woman was never discovered although in the Rockies it could be anywhere. We could give Rob Caulfield the benefit of the doubt but, if people had, there wouldn't have been just me from the DA's office at his book launch. Rob liked to be the hero. What I didn't realise until he told me the tale about Carol Hunnicut, and he never told it the same way twice, was how much.

NEIL McCAULEY

HEAT
USA 1995
DIRECTOR – MICHAEL MANN

I've told you everything I know. How many times do I have to tell you, Detective Hanna? What's the point? The men are all dead. You heard the witnesses. The news was all over the TV. There's nothing to tell. I don't know anything about any robber that escaped. Aren't you tired? I'm tired. I'm really tired. I also have a thirst. Yes, a coffee would be fine. Thank you. No, I don't eat donuts. No, thank you. If you want, if I have to, I'll start again. You can tell me if I miss anything this time. Wouldn't that be nice? You must know all this better than me.

I met Neil McCauley in a restaurant while I was on my lunch break. The place was crowded, and he sat down next to me. He was reading a book. I like that, people who sit in public places and read, people who don't need to talk all the time. I had seen him before in the bookshop where I worked. He never spoke to anyone, mumbled thank you when he bought a book. I was curious about him. He didn't look like a typical customer. I was used to shy men in bookshops but Neil had confidence as well as his streak of shyness. He was quiet and without fear. I was more curious than interested. You understand me, Detective Hanna?

Because I was and had been curious, I asked him what he was reading. I didn't ask him what he was eating. I asked him what he was reading. Neil was annoyed that I had interrupted his lunch. He was sharp with me to be honest but then I told him I'd seen him in the bookshop and he apologised and we talked. I think he was flattered that I remembered him. I did most of the talking. Neil asked a lot of questions, always. I liked the way he listened and waited for me to finish. I'd never met a man who asked so many questions and was so attentive. He was older than me but that wasn't a problem. It might have been if he'd been a selfish man but he wasn't. I talked, and he listened. But what we had wasn't all about me. I felt something for him.

Until that day of the bank robbery I had no idea he was a criminal. I thought he was a salesman like he said. I don't like salesmen usually but Neil read books and he appeared to be interested in what he said he sold. What? He said he sold solid metals. I knew nothing about stuff like that. I do think he had a curious mind. I told myself he had. Neil had a good memory. He remembered everything I said. We were a pair of home birds. We had quiet evenings. I would play a CD, and we would both read. Men who are mysterious are much more attractive than men that you know. Neil was too quiet to be a salesman. I should have realised.

Thank you. Are you sure this is coffee? My God, no, I don't want any sugar. He didn't mention you, Detective Hanna. Other than his family he didn't mention anyone, ever. His mother had died, his father had absconded, and he had lost touch with his brother. Neil said that, being a salesman, he was too busy working to make friends. I did wonder about that but I liked the quiet life, and you believe what you want to believe. He didn't want to meet my friends but neither was he possessive. I put that down to him being quiet and shy. I liked him being like that because of what I do in my spare time as a graphic designer. With a lot of my friends I am hustling for work. I wanted to keep that stuff private. The people I know talk a lot.

Neil was generous. He had a fine apartment, and I spent a lot of time there. I kept my own place. If he had been younger, I might have given up my apartment. I suppose I must have had some doubts about him. There are days when you appreciate the remoteness but there are moments when you wonder. You understand me? Are you married, Detective Hanna? I'm sorry. I wouldn't have asked if I'd known.

NEIL McCAULEY

Is that right? I didn't even know he'd been in prison, never mind two of them. I'm just thinking, sorry. What kind of mark does that leave on a man, and what kind of man is prepared to go to prison? Everything about Neil was so precise and neat, not just him being tidy. Neil could sit still all night if he had to, read his book and not even move in his armchair. But if he did anything, it was like he had it timed to the split second. I found that attractive. No, I'm not like that either, Detective Hanna. You spill things as well. We have something in common then.

I didn't know other people set up jobs for him. Is that how it works? Well, I didn't know that. I don't mix with criminals. When I was waiting for Neil and sitting in the car I wasn't thinking about how he did his work. No, I thought about the poor people who had been killed in the bank robbery. And how he lived with it, and how in the future I would have to. Neil said the killings were in self-defence and wouldn't have happened if there hadn't been policemen too ready to fire. I sat there thinking about what had happened and wondering just why I was there in the car waiting for a man that I knew nothing about but a man I was as close to as anyone I had ever known. Are these what you want to see, Detective Hanna, my tears? Yes, thank you, a tissue would be fine. No, not another coffee.

Neil said we could have a new life in New Zealand. He would set me up with a new studio for my graphic design work. He mentioned New Zealand a lot. He had this idea that the States was a dirty wreck of a country and that New Zealand would be fresh and clean. Neil said it would be a good place for the two of us to grow old. I thought it might be, the two of us getting old and staying in love and breathing fresh air. I didn't know it was just his escape route, nothing more. I feel such a fool now. But I also hate the idea of him being dead. I hope he died thinking it was worth it. I spoke to him that day in the restaurant because I was lonely. Neil wanted fresh New Zealand air, and I wanted a quiet clean man.

I remember one day when it was my turn to ask Neil questions. I asked him why he sold solid metals. Just listen to me. It doesn't even make any sense. Nobody makes a living selling solid metals. But we believe what we want to believe. Neil said he did what he did best and that he wouldn't want to do anything else. I thought it was an odd thing for a salesman to say. He also told me he had this dream of drowning and that he would die in the middle of the dream and not wake up. I remember him waking up in a cold sweat and me hugging him back to sleep.

Maybe that was why I was waiting in the car. I thought that whatever he'd done he would need me. After he told me about the bank robbery I ran away and Neil chased me and dragged me back. Later, he said I could go. But by then I had changed my mind. Neil said he didn't want to go anywhere without me but I could leave if I wanted. I let him hug me and I felt that he was all that I am or would be. He was the missing jigsaw puzzle for me. My other half, you know, like in the play by Plato. That was why I waited in the car outside the hotel and stayed there even after the fire alarm which I realised was something to do with Neil. I told myself there was no alternative to us being together. It was just the way it is. But then Neil walks out of the hotel wearing a hotel uniform and he walks straight past me. And I realised that's all I was, an alternative and that the next woman he meets will be just another alternative. Maybe that's all we ever are, alternatives to what could have been. You understand me, Detective Hanna? You've been married how many times? If you've had three wives, you should know about alternatives. I can't drink this coffee. Is it possible to have a glass of water?

Detective Hanna, you remind me of Neil, all this talking I've been doing and you just sitting there, asking questions and listening like he used to. You say you want to find the missing robber and that there are other accomplices but you look to me as if you're just curious about what Neil was like. What am I going to do next? Oh, I'll go home. I assume I can go home. I'll try and relax and do some design work. A couple of my designs have been used on CDs. It's not work I can live on. At some point I'll make myself a decent coffee and think about starting again, I suppose. Work, relax, phone my mother, think about what's happened. It's not as if I don't have alternatives. What are you going to next, Detective Hanna, now Neil is dead? What are your alternatives?

KEYSER SÖZE

THE USUAL SUSPECTS
USA 1995
DIRECTOR – BRYAN SINGER

Let me look at that picture again. Man, I was something. Forget? I remember everything. Look, there in the picture, look at the pistol on the hip next to the braces. People copied me but I was the first. I was forty three years old and making a name for myself in US Customs. That was one expensive suit. My wife picked my clothes and she liked the trousers to hang right, so I wore braces. I was in shape. I still work out but I've just had my sixty-eighth birthday. These days I think more about the big seven-zero. My wife loved buying clothes. She still likes buying clothes but that's another story.

Look, see how Rabin wrote my name on the back of the photo, DAVE KUJAN, BIG SHOT. He was being cute. Rabin never made it past Detective Sergeant. But he had an office and the dope was happy. People say Keyser Söze was why my career stalled. I don't think so. My level was sharp suits, a pistol and braces. I was no big boss man. I wanted to be the strong hero fighting the bad men. Now, I wish I'd thought more about promotion and had a bigger pension except that's not true either. I have more green stuff than I can spend and a house with a swimming pool that at my age I don't need to be bigger.

But you brought me the picture, and I'll be straight with you. Dave Kujan, big shot, was never the same after that day with Keyser Söze. I spoke to him for just two hours. One hundred and twenty minutes, and without the creep moving from the chair where he sat he changed my life. I was different after Keyser Söze. See, I used to divide people into the strong and weak. The strong looked good, had willpower and courage. They were also smart. The strong had good suits. The weak were, well, they weren't any of that. The guy I interrogated was one of the weak, so I thought, a pathetic piece of trash. About Verbal, I was wrong big style.

Dean Keaton was one of the strong. He was one step ahead. Keaton wore good suits, and people died around him. Not because of the suits, because of him. This was why I had to nail Dean Keaton. I understood. If he won, I would be weaker, and if I won, I would be stronger. I thought like that in those days. Then Keyser or Verbal or Roger or whatever he was called walked free. These days I've no idea what is strong or weak. I couldn't tell you what kind of man I am or what I amount to. These days I help out in a post-traumatic stress clinic. It's not too far from here. Those guys know what it's like to have dark days, and so do I.

But you're not here to know about me. You want to know all about Keyser Söze. Do I have regrets? Well, it may have taken me time to recover from what happened but that day I don't regret. I met a good friend in Detective Sergeant Jeff Rabin and I never forgot something he said to me after Keyser walked.

Stand back and always see the bigger picture, said Jeff.

And since then, and perhaps since Keyser or Verbal, I always have tried to see things from a distance.

If only I had stood back that day. I was so close and too close. I ran into that office thinking this was my chance to nail a rat called Dean Keaton. The terrible truth is I wanted Keaton and lost Keyser Söze, a guy who had been wandering around a ship killing people at random. Twenty seven people died that day in San Pedro Bay.

Jeff is a good friend but I still curse him for not letting me use one of the interrogation rooms. Jeff said the rooms were bugged, and, like a clown, I went along with him. But those guys were cops that bent the rules. I was a law enforcement officer with US Customs. I followed rules. That was how the Agency worked. I should have insisted to Jeff. Sometimes I tell myself that without what was in the room the lies from Verbal would have been different and he wouldn't have kidded me. Everyone knows how he picked the names off the wall behind Jeff's desk. I bet you know. That's right. Only Jeff, Keyser and me were in that room but everybody is an expert. The Skokie barbershop quartet and Redfoot the lawyer he invented off the top of his head. He sees the name Guatemala somewhere and he talks about how he used to pick coffee beans. What was the point? He told lies when he didn't have to. He even used the name off the bottom of my coffee mug for Kobayashi, the man who was supposed to set up the big deal. What would have Keyser said in an interrogation room without anything on the walls. I wonder. Well, I did at first. I was there to be suckered. I wanted Keaton too much. I was a strong man who wanted to be stronger and Verbal, Keyser or whatever, knew it.

You know, you only survived in my job if you assumed everyone was a liar. You didn't always get it right. The people you thought were lying did sometimes tell the truth. I had bad experiences but never because I reckoned some guy or dame was straight and honest. That's how it had to be. Verbal had been around the block. He knew how I was programmed. Verbal was talking to a man that wanted to hear lies he could break down. Because I was desperate, lies about Keaton were even better. He let me think I'd won. That's how a con works. You can only hook someone who thinks he's a wise guy. I learnt a lot that day.

Verbal was famous as a low grade conman but even that was a con. Keyser Söze had an empire, so why he went around pretending to be small time and getting arrested for it is beyond me. I'm not wrong. That's what he did. He had a charge sheet as Roger 'Verbal' Kint. I saw it the night we pulled them in for the line-up. I suppose it meant we always looked elsewhere which is of course what we did that day.

Yes, I heard that. I don't know how that story got around. Verbal told me all about the supposed heist in the car park but he never said he killed Saul Berg. Why would he? He was pretending to be pathetic. That stuff has been added by others to make a good story.

This is where we are. People adding nonsense to something that began as nothing but lies. No, you are right, there was some truth in there. If only we knew how much, eh? This is what I know and this is why you are here, right?

The line-up happened. Of course it did. I helped lift Dean Keaton the same night. That was one sweet moment. You should have seen his face, in front of his so smart dame. Keaton with his fancy friends and pretending to be a legit businessman. What happened to McManus, Keaton and Hockney we'll never know. The cops assumed that those three perished in San Pedro Bay in the attack that happened on the boat but that could have been lies. I've no idea who helped Verbal kill stool pigeon Arturo Marquez that night in the Bay. And was Fenster dead before what happened in the Bay like Verbal said or did he die in the Bay? If Fenster was buried on a beach like Verbal said, he must now be under the rocks somewhere. The body never floated up anywhere.

I can only tell you what I know. The lineup happened. So did the raid on the New York cops. Fifty three were hounded out of the force. The scandal was all over the press. And Keyser Söze existed because a Hungarian mobster on his deathbed told FBI man Jeff Baer. And the description of Keyser Söze matched Verbal but I didn't need to see a drawing on the fax to know that. Arturo Marquez was no fake name Verbal saw on a wall. Arturo was a big informer for the FBI, a real catch. I know because I read the Bureau report. And we all know somebody wanted to kill Marquez because some sharpshooter shot him through the temple. Bang went a witness.

Did we find ninety three million dollars? There was a lot of money but the bread was nearer ninety one million. This was the docks, and you know what happens. There was also a ruined boat and that was not cheap. Are Keaton, McManus and Hockney still out there? I've heard nothing. There are rumours about Keyser Söze but no more than that. The last one I heard was that he was living the high life in Brazil and doing corrupt deals with the politicians.

Jack Baer was lucky. FBI boys know how to keep their shoes clean, and Jack was no exception. Jack was in the harbour and far away from Verbal. Not so lucky, though, as it happened. The big boys did Jack Baer for corruption. Afterwards Jack only goes to Albuquerque and reinvents himself as a Chilean and builds this crystal meth empire. Poacher turned gamekeeper, eh? It all came out a couple of years ago. Some schoolteacher who was also making crystal meth blew Jack's head off his shoulders. But that's another story. A Chilean, dammit. Jack didn't even look South American. Look, you should talk to Jeff Rabin.

SYDNEY

HARD EIGHT
USA 1996
DIRECTOR – PAUL THOMAS ANDERSON

Like, I thought Sydney had cancer, the way he looked and everything. Not that he ever had looked good. Sydney had these bags under his eyes that reached half-way down his face. I saw Sydney the week before he died. The guy wanted to talk, needed I suppose, except he could hardly breathe. He had this emphysomething, that's it, emphysema. Sydney always liked the nicotine. I liked the way he smoked. Sydney had a neat way with a cigarette. All in all, he was a neat guy. He was not so tall, not as tall as me. I'm tall for a woman but only a little tall. Short or not, Sydney talked like he was above us all, even down there where he was. The man didn't talk so much. All I remember is him giving orders. God knows, Sydney had cause.

The visit to the hospital was the first time I'd seen Sydney since the night in the motel when John and me messed up. That night was the one time Sydney lost his temper. In the afternoon John had proposed to me and I said yes. I only met the guy the night before but I thought why not. John was clean and polite and he knew Sydney. Girls who've never been in the business can't understand why I did a trick on my wedding night. A businessman offered me three hundred dollars, and it was an opportunity, so I said yes.

The problem was the creep didn't want to pay. I always carry these handcuffs in my bag, you know, some men like that sort of thing. The guy was loaded and arguing how he didn't need to pay especially as he had lost so much at the tables. This was when I cooed something in his ear and slipped a handcuff on his wrist and fastened the slob to the bed. I told the guy his wife would have to cough up the dough. The guy said no way was he calling his wife and telling her he was being held hostage for three hundred bucks by a hooker. So I called John and asked him to come over. After John roughed him up the guy called his wife and said she had to bring the money.

The wife still didn't turn up, so John hit the man again but it made no difference. I screamed a few times, and that didn't help any either. Some of these guys have no shame. The john on the bed, not my John, groans and bleeds some more, and we wait. My John has a pal called Jimmy who is this black guy running security at the hotel where I work as a waitress. Jimmy arrives because John calls him but all Jimmy does is say wait for the wife to pay what's owed. John tells Jimmy that the wife doesn't want to hand over three hundred bucks because she doesn't think it right that she should be paying for her husband banging a hooker.

Get rid of the guy then, says Jimmy.

Kill him? says John.

Why not? says Jimmy.

And I say, Pardon me, what about my three hundred bucks and how about fair is fair?

Jimmy just grins and walks out the door. John has this puzzled look on his face the frequency of which recently I have to admit has begun to annoy me.

What about my three hundred bucks, I say, is anybody listening to me? This is when John calls Sydney, the man who looks out for him and has done since Sydney found John sitting against the wall of some diner and with nowhere to go. Sydney arrives and is soon giving orders.

I say, Sydney, what about my three hundred bucks?

He says, what the hell.

And Sydney starts talking about how this is kidnapping and how that this guy bleeding and handcuffed to the bed is one serious business and we should be worrying about a lot more than three hundred bucks. The guy is just handcuffed to the bed is all.

I've lost count of the number of guys I've handcuffed to a bed. I don't say this to Sydney and John. Sydney pushes John and me out the room and into some car and makes sure that we get the hell out of Reno. John agrees with Sydney to take me to Niagara Falls.

Have yourselves a honeymoon, says Sydney.

This is a good idea I think, especially as Sydney gives John some money to pay for things and promises to send us more cash when we need it which he did, for a while at least.

The money helps John and me to settle down in Idaho. John forgets the casinos, and I don't turn no tricks no more. John now works in a car repair shop and does local deliveries. I work in a coffee shop but all the guys want are breakfasts and apple pie. John and me live in a real quiet town. The life in Reno and Vegas I put behind me. I made my mind up to do this at Niagara. The sight of all that water affects you. I wanted the rest of my life to be clean. And then I get this phone call to say Sydney was in hospital, didn't have long left and wanted to talk to me. I was surprised, I can tell you. Most of the time Sydney just gave John and me orders.

I see Sydney in the hospital, and he looks and sounds terrible. He is sitting up straight in this hospital bed. These giant pillows are bright white, and his face is as grey as a bad Idaho sky before it pours down, of which I have seen plenty. I cried just at the sight of him, and, typical Sydney, he tells me to shut up straight away.

I have to talk to someone, he says.

You should talk to John, I say, seeing how you looked after him for so long.

This can't be said to John, he says.

Sydney pulls on my arm and says how Jimmy said something to him, Sydney, the night before he, Jimmy, died. Now at this point I say nothing because I know Jimmy was plugged and I have a strong suspicion that Sydney was the man that did the plugging, especially with what I know about Jimmy and John.

Sydney is struggling for breath but he tells me that Jimmy knew about how Sydney had shot John's old man in the face and killed him and that this was why Sydney looked out for John.

Why are you telling me this? I say to Sydney.

If anyone tells John, you have to tell him it's not true. You tell John, says Sydney, that you saw me on my deathbed and I denied killing his father and that I insisted and you believed me. Can you say all that, Clementine? he says.

I know. I hate my stupid name. And he grabs my hand so tight that I think he's going to die with him holding on to me and they'll have to drag him off.

Sure, sure, I say.

I kiss the top off his head and somehow that convinces him. I knew he was dying right then because his hair tasted funny. Even now it makes me feel queasy to remember.

Of course, I do not tell Sydney that Jimmy had told me the tale well before John and me left Reno and how John has known for some time because I told him but that John figured that Sydney was old and those things were in the past and, whatever went down, Sydney had always been good to us. Sydney talks more.

I'm in the mood to confess, says Sydney.

I ain't no priest, I say.

I ain't no Catholic, says Sydney. I don't want no priest. All my life I've had to be the guy who's had to fix things. Even as a kid.

And then Sydney stops and bends his head forward.

I know who did it, he says.

Did what? I say.

I was a kid of sixteen and working in the Astor Motel, says Sydney. I kept the forecourt clean and the drinks machines stocked. I saw them arrive, these two men and a woman. This was back in 1947. One of the guys had a limousine and dressed like a movie star. The girl was a dark haired beauty.

The next day they were all gone but Henry Hoffman who ran the motel came up to me and said, You have to help me, Sydney. Something has happened in Cabin 3.

The cabin where the beauty stayed, I said.

She's gone, Sydney, but there's, well there's a lot of stuff left.

Stuff, I said.

Blood and stuff, said Mr Hoffman.

You can guess, Clementine, says Sydney to me. The deal was I would clean Cabin 3 but, if anyone asked, I was not in that day. So I held my nose, cleaned the cabin, and Mr Hoffman paid me overtime. I said nothing to anyone but the LAPD turned up and asked around after Mr Hoffman had decided to tell people what had happened. He sure took his time making his mind up. Mr Hoffman said he cleaned the room but, yes, there had been blood and stuff in the room that day. The two men I had seen were known to the police but no one was charged.

Typical LAPD, said Mr Hoffman.

The woman I had seen in that cabin I saw later in the newspapers but there was no mention of her ever being in the Astor Motel, says Sydney.

Sydney takes a deep breath and his chest rattles like a steam train. He smiles at me and despite the wrinkles he looks like a little kid.

The murder the Press boys wrote about had a special name, says Sydney. You won't remember, Clementine.

Well, I say, what did they call it?

The Black Dahlia murder, says Sydney.

Sydney was old and tired but excited. He grabbed my arm, and I felt his bony fingers and remembered when Sydney used to give orders. He struggled for breath.

Clementine, he said, the killer was a guest at the Astor Motel, and what's more the cops knew it. But the killer had a friend called Hansen, Mark Marinus Hansen. This Hanson dude threw big parties in LA. He had friends and influence everywhere. Listen to this, Clementine.

He was coughing by now.

Listen, Clementine, this bigwig called Hansen had the cops pulled off the case.

I smiled at Sydney. I didn't like to see him coughing. His lungs wheezed like something else. I think it was his breathing that made him whisper and pull me down to his ear.

I saw the killer, Clementine, he said. He was a Norwegian looking guy.

Sydney whispered the name in my ear. I hardly felt his breath but I just about heard the name.

Leslie Duane Dillon, said Sydney. He had this Adam's apple that stuck out. Clementine, I'll never forget that guy.

Those were the last words he said. You could say my visit to the hospital was a waste of time. John knew about Sydney and his father already, and I have other things to worry about besides some damned murder from over sixty years ago.

Lightning Source UK Ltd.
Milton Keynes UK
UKHW020752231220
375771UK00007B/101